ARSENAL

MEMORIES AND MARBLE HALLS

ARSENAL

MEMORIES AND MARBLE HALLS

DAVID SIMS

First published in Great Britain in 2000 by
PAVILION BOOKS LIMITED
London House, Great Eastern Wharf, Parkgate
Road, London SW11 4NQ
www.pavilionbooks.co.uk

Designed by Nigel Partridge
Editorial consultant: Nick Mason

A CIP catalogue record for this book is
available from the British Library.

ISBN 1 86205 427 4

Set in Univers and Bembo

Colour reproduction by Conti Tipocolor
Printed and bound in Italy by Conti Tipocolor

1 3 5 7 9 10 8 6 4 2

This book may be ordered by post direct from
the publisher. Please contact the Marketing
Department. But try your bookshop first.

CONTENTS

ACKNOWLEDGEMENTS

My thanks to all the people associated with this project. Without their help and encouragement this book would probably have just remained an ambitious thought. Thanks to my mother, who introduced me to the Arsenal; to my father, who first took me to a game; to Paola, who shares the experiences in the North Bank; and to my friends around the world, *the* Highbury faithful. My love to Siobhan, for the long hours reading and transcribing the many letters and text. And thanks to everyone at Arsenal Football Club, John Hazell, Peter Smith, Daniel Flesch, and Dan Tolhurst – it has been a memorable experience not just compiling this book but also meeting and working with you.

But thanks most of all to every Arsenal supporter who took the time to write their own personal memories and look out their wonderful photographs, and allow us all to share them. This is their book.

FOREWORD BY PETER HILL-WOOD

CHAIRMAN, ARSENAL FOOTBALL CLUB

Memories and Marble Halls creates a momentous time capsule for Arsenal's many supporters all around the world at the beginning of a new millennium.

The idea of collecting photographs and stories together from fans is not a new one, but their selection and treatment by David Sims – himself a lifelong Arsenal fan – shows the passion and love we all know exists at the heart of our great club. The range and detail of the images, which have been submitted from all over the globe, are really fascinating.

The illustration of Arsenal's history from the supporters' perspective is something truly special. We all have deeply ingrained reminiscences from the game of football, and this book contains a host of anecdotes that awaken memories for me and my family, just as I am sure they will for so many families with Arsenal in their blood, inspired by sheer enthusiasm for the club handed down from generation to generation.

With my own family's historical involvement in Arsenal Football Club, I naturally have many fond memories since my introduction as a child to the Marble Halls of Highbury. I have seen many great players and performances over the years, a lot of which are covered in detail in the book. Like all other supporters, I have great memories of our major triumphs over the years, with the two Double-winning seasons of 1970/1 and 1997/98, together with the dramatic League Championship triumph in 1989, among the best of them.

I found the Behind Highbury sections and David Sims' match day photographs of particular interest. To look down on the stadium from the roof of the North Bank is a unique sight and confirms the great work done by Steve Braddock and his ground staff. The catalogue of images from match day almost make you feel the atmosphere as kick-off approaches. And the fans' own photographs bear witness to a lifetime's journey for the Arsenal supporter. They act as a visual record of fan and club through the decades, and create a collector's item for everyone, young and old.

Arsenal has formed an enviable reputation for taking the lead on the national and international stage. This book has once again set the precedent. I hope you enjoy it as much as I have.

* Peter Hill-Wood has been Arsenal's chairman since 1982, following his father Denis Hill-Wood (chairman 1961-82) and his grandfather Samuel Hill-Wood, who became chairman in the late 1920's.

INTRODUCTION

Bergkamp, Wright, Overmars, Merson – what a decade the Nineties were! "Kanu, Kanu, Kaaaa-nuuu" – remember them all? The midfield hunters, Petit and Vieira – the greatest partnership in history!"

"No way. What about Ted Drake and Cliff Bastin in the Thirties?"

"Oh yeah, right, like I remember them. Do you?"

"Nah… but I've read about 'em…"

"Well, don't forget the back five: Seaman, Dixon, Winterburn, Keown and Captain Arsenal himself – Tony Adams."

"Stevie Bould, he's got no hair, Steve-y Bould!"

"What memories, eh?"

"Yeah, what a decade that was, after we beat the scousers."

"Now that was a night, I tell you…"

"What about the Nineties Double? Now that was a night!"

This conversation takes place thirty years from now, in a pub somewhere in North London. Two Arsenal supporters, looking back with fondness and admiration to the glorious Nineties.

Memories and Marble Halls is compiled from such memories, memories shared from before the famous Thirties all the way through to those triumphant days as the century closed. These are the real stories – written and told by Arsenal supporters the way they saw and experienced them. Share their deeply personal letters, photographs, and anecdotes on the club and team. Share too their emotions – all those emotions you have felt following the Arsenal.

As we enter a new millennium, we capture a moment in time for Arsenal Football Club. A lot has changed since the 1930s for the supporter, more quickly in the last ten years, after Hillsborough and the Taylor report than in the last fifty. We've seen the introduction of all-seater stadiums, live televised games and increased ticket prices, and we have all felt these changes shaping our lives. The development of football and its social acceptance is told inadvertently by the supporters' letters. Their very language, their changing use of words and phrases through the decades, subtly show football's social evolution. We read with complete affinity the way the "beautiful game" has evolved along with the Arsenal supporter.

What was once a working man's pastime has developed over the years. There have been many highs and lows – two world wars, hooliganism, tragic accidents, ground developments, championships and Doubles. But football remains today what it always should be: a day to share with family and friends… and, of course, your fellow Gooners.

You know that you will never forget your first game, first trophy, first away game. Win or lose, it is the memories that you take away from the match after the final whistle, along with your programme. These memories grow to mean

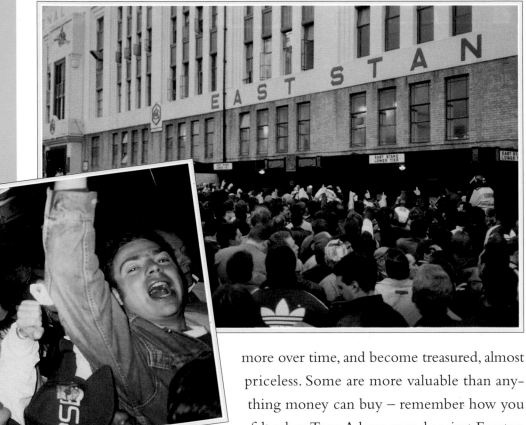

more over time, and become treasured, almost priceless. Some are more valuable than anything money can buy – remember how you felt when Tony Adams scored against Everton and picked up the Premiership trophy in '98? Or Michael Thomas lobbed Grobbelaar in '89?

Poignant moments, humour that almost hurts, intense personal emotion and, every so often, euphoria can all occur on the same day while watching a game of football. So just imagine what could be built up over a lifetime of supporting the Arse. The passing years only serve to ingrain these memories more deeply, memories that resurface without warning in our daily lives when we're away from the Arsenal.

Even during the close season the

supporter never switches off – there is always some news to follow. Who will be signed? Who will be sold? What about the new fixtures…

Over the years Arsenal has welcomed supporters worldwide. With the foreign players now in the squad, fans come from all over the globe to see their stars. For some supporters it is difficult to get to the games, but they still follow them on television or via the internet while far away from Highbury – perhaps even abroad, where I'll bet you have found yourself scouring the local press for results in a language you haven't a hope in hell of understanding… But, when you come to think about it, "one-nil to the Arsenal" is the same in any language in the world.

DAVID SIMS
London, December 1999

THE EARLY YEARS

"I DREAMT THAT I DWELT IN MARBLE HALLS"

The first match Arsenal played at Highbury was against Leicester Fosse, on 6th September 1913; they won 2–1. At that time they were still officially known as Woolwich Arsenal. The following year that would all change: on 3rd April 1914 the club was renamed simply *The Arsenal*.

After the move from Woolwich to Highbury, the huge banks that the supporters first stood on were formed with the soil left over from the digging of Gillespie Road Underground station, which had opened seven years earlier. It would be nearly twenty years before the station would adopt its present name – Arsenal.

So finally Highbury started to take shape. The West Stand, designed by Claude Ferrier, was built in 1932 and opened on 10th December by The Prince of Wales. Across the pitch was left the rickety old wooden East Stand, and that too was earmarked for a revamp. The same architect was chosen to design its replacement, and

his plans were accepted; sadly both he and the manager Herbert Chapman had died before its inauguration on 24th October 1936.

The public saw it as "state of the art" – a masterpiece of the art deco style so fashionable in the 1930s. The building costs were £130,000 – a snip in today's financial climate, but in 1930s' Britain a huge amount of money. Certainly no football stadium in the land could stand comparison with Highbury, and with the opening of both stands Arsenal's place on the world stage was assured.

It was nearly sixty years later, in 1993, that the new North Bank opened – costing £16 million and incorporating a new museum. Its curator, Iain Cook,

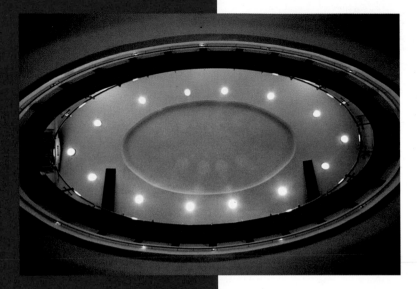

ABOVE
High above the heads of the North Bank fans, the entrance to the Arsenal Museum.

a fixture at Arsenal for over twenty years, explains: "Many of the exhibits were gathered from supporters, and added to the extensive collection Arsenal already had. Sadly, with so many old programmes and books, it is difficult to display them all, so we keep them stored in a library."

A rotational system allows a huge array of pieces to be viewed over a season by the visitor. "It's only open on Fridays, and on match days to North Bank ticket holders. But we have a very successful stadium tour operation that keeps the numbers topped up." He estimates that the annual attendance at the museum is around 15,000. To add to the attraction, a cinema in the museum shows *The Arsenal History* – from 1886, a film updated regularly with each year's history-making memories.

"It keeps us very busy, especially when Arsenal keep on winning trophies."

And what of the Marble Halls? Even for those who knew only one phrase of the immensely popular Victorian ballad, "I dreamt that I dwelt in marble halls With vassals and serfs at my side," it must have been a familiar metaphor for

RIGHT
Main landing, East Stand, in the 1930s.

ABOVE
*High in the East Stand –
the bar was the longest in
Thirties Britain.*

grandeur and opulence, and the new East Stand would certainly have given that impression in its early days. The image may have lost some of its universal impact – "Quite often today people look into the stand and say 'Ah, so this is the Marble Hall' – it's not quite what they expect" – but in the Thirties it would have been a sensation.

Who actually lifted the line from The Bohemian Girl and attached it to Arsenal's new pride and joy is not known, but the prime suspect is George Allison. He had been a commentator and a radio personality since the medium's early days (he had commentated on the Arsenal-Cardiff Cup Final of 1927 with commendable impartiality), and he had even become a director of the club. But when Herbert Chapman died so suddenly the club decided to give the personality his chance. It worked out well: he was probably the first team manager

RIGHT

The 1930s cocktail bar –
now transformed into the
club's offices.

BELOW

"History of Arsenal"
Cinema.

to speak out and talk easily to the press, and he also realised the potential of good public relations at a time when other managers were pretty quiet. They knew all about the running of their clubs, but they had little to do with the individual players; they tended just to tell them who was in the team, and off they went.

But Chapman had changed all that.

Anyway, the East Stand was completed about a year after Allison had succeeded to the job, and it would be no surprise if the tongue-in-cheek idea to christen his workplace the Marble Halls had been his.

Iain has a lot of questions asked, too, about the use of the ground during the Second World War. "During the war Arsenal played their home games at Tottenham, with Highbury commandeered as an Air Raid Precautions site. It was originally to have been an ambulance clearing station but luckily there was no heavy bombing in the Highbury area. The North Bank roof was burnt off one day, simply because they were storing loads of bunk beds under it; an incendiary bomb got through and the whole lot went up."

It's often stated that Arsenal lost more players during the War than any other club. "In a sense that was true, but it is also true that a great number of players

from all over the country were connected to the club at that time – even Bill Shankly played a few games for Arsenal. He happened to be stationed in London for a few months and just turned up and played. In fact Arsenal had many wartime guest players, including Stanley Matthews and Stan Mortensen.

"When the League began again after the war, the use of guest players was stopped, and you had to use players officially on the books. The problem with that was that the club didn't get any younger players coming through, so you find that certainly in the late Forties and early Fifties the players were getting quite old. They were in their late 30s and even their early 40s simply because the war had got in the way, and there were no younger players developing through the youth system. Eventually that changed, but Joe Mercer was still playing at 39. Now we have Nigel Winterburn and Lee Dixon – but the precedent was set then for very different reasons.

"For some players, like Cliff Bastin and Ted Drake, their careers were hampered by the war. There is no denying that Ian Wright broke Bastin's record, but had the war not come along, who knows how many more goals Bastin would have scored."

One of Iain's most moving stories comes from the other world war. "During February 1916, Bob Benson turned up for an away game in Reading. He had played a few games with Arsenal before the war, but he had gone into ammunition work away from Highbury. On that day the team were a player short, and they asked him to play. Bob had not had a game for about a year and a half, and had let his fitness drop. He played for about forty minutes trying to keep up with the game, but began to feel unwell. He left the pitch and at half time, and sadly he died – the one player in Arsenal colours to actually die in the dressing room. He was later buried in his Arsenal shirt."

Iain's most prized exhibits are Charlie George's double-winning medals and Herbert Chapman's bowler hat – "a real one off", the curator says proudly.

"But everyone who visits has his or her own particular favourite, depending on what team, player or era they are into."

His favourite personal memory of working at Highbury was Arsenal's League Championship victory in 1989. "The staff had all worked that day and we couldn't make the trip up north, so we hired a big television for the East Stand. When Arsenal went one–nil up we all felt we had done really well, and decided we would have the champagne and just say 'Bad luck, guys, but well done.' Then when Michael Thomas scored the winner all hell broke loose.

"Within twenty minutes the crowds were outside in the street. It was like the end of *Fever Pitch*, but with hundreds more people. At that time they were ren-

ABOVE
*Memorabilia on display in
the museum.*

20

ovating the East Stand and it had scaffolding all over it. One Arsenal chap actually climbed all the way up the scaffolding to the top of the stand and stuck up a flag – he had made it at home in a hurry with "Champions" written on it. He was apprehended later, still suffering from shock, and only then realised what a dangerous climb he had just completed. Luckily for him he wasn't charged.

"We all stayed around till four or five in the morning. It was a lively evening, with Highbury being the focal point. Most people were still in shock themselves. They just needed to congregate together for it all to sink in. Most of them had expected the worst but we had won 2–0, and the team were coming home with the Championship."

A TIME TO REMEMBER...

EMILIO ZORLAKKI
Pilgrimage to Plumstead

Before you get too confused, let me inform you that I am standing on the terrace steps from our old Invicta Ground in Plumstead, which is situated in Hector Street. It was Arsenal's home between 1890 and 1893.

The picture was taken in about April 1997, when a group of Arsenal devotees and historians decided to go on a pilgrimage to Woolwich Arsenal and Plumstead, in search of "our roots". On our day out, we also decided to call in at the public house *Royal Oak*, where Dial Square was formed.

There are three or four houses in Hector Street which still have the old terraced steps in the back gardens. We think this is an archaeological phenomenon (well, can't help being biased). You'll be hard pressed to find any monument or building connected with Arsenal as old as this.

ROBERT COOKE
The high and the low

Although my son and I are long distance Gooners I thought you would like a few lines as to how we ended up supporting this great club. Also, as I am sure you are well aware, the year 2000 marks an historic milestone in the history of Arsenal Football Club – for it was on 12th March 1900 that Arsenal recorded their record victory, 12–0 v Loughborough Town.

Although I have been a regular at Highbury for the past 30-odd years, I am still asked the same old question, why do I support Arsenal – who are 110 miles away? The answer is quite simple. My late father was an avid Arsenal fan from childhood, and it was he who introduced my brother and me to the Gunners – the names of Bastin, Drake, Hapgood and James were often recalled with pride.

As youngsters my brother and I were confined to away games only. Leicester, Notts Forest and Derby were only 15 miles away. But it was always a thrill when Saturday came and we could go and watch our idols, who in those barren 1960s were a bit thin on the ground. Nonetheless, I saw some great players – Joe Baker, George Eastham, Geoff Strong – my only regret was that I never saw the late great Jack Kelsey. We tended to lose quite a few times to the clubs I have mentioned but we enjoyed every minute.

I can remember during the Sixties a chap in white trousers and red waistcoat sporting a top hat with an Arsenal rosette walking round the pitch with a banner proclaiming, "We Arsenal supporters say may the best team win".

As I reached the age of 15, I started work and recall my very first visit to the home of football. Arsenal were due to play Nottingham Forest on 23rd December 1967 and the day before the match a Forest fan asked if I wanted a lift in his car. As you can imagine I jumped at the chance. I didn't sleep a wink that Friday night thinking about it.

We stood on the West Terrace and the day ended in perfection: 3–0 to Arsenal. George Graham scored two and Geordie Armstrong one. I still have the programme, price 6d (2½p). That was it – hooked on the Gunners! My son Darran now follows Arsenal. Mind you, he was introduced to Highbury much earlier than I was, although it wasn't such a pleasing result – Arsenal 1 Watford 3 in a 1987 FA Cup tie. He hasn't had a bad few years since, though, has he?

We are both Season Ticket holders now in the Clock End, and also go to all away matches. Most of our journeys to Highbury are made by train from Loughborough. It is on the walk to the station that we pass a pub called the *Greyhound Hotel*, not a remarkable piece of architecture by any means, but it does have a large slice of Arsenal history attached to it. For it was here, behind the pub that Arsenal suffered their worst ever defeat in their proud history, losing 8–0 to Loughborough Town in a Division Two league match on 12th December 1896.

However, revenge was not far away – and on 12th March 1900 Arsenal mercilessly gunned down the Town 12–0 at Plumstead to complete a unique double – Arsenal being the only club to record a record defeat and victory against the same club.

BELOW
The Greyhound, Loughborough.

BELOW

*Jimmy Dunne runs out of
the tunnel as Graham's
grandad Henry Agent is
seen in the left corner – to
the right of the man
holding the white card. His
brother Rubin Agent is in
the front row on the left of
the two women.*

GRAHAM BARBER

The face by the tunnel

I have been an Arsenal fan for as long as I can remember, being introduced to Arsenal by my grandad, Henry Agent. He originally lived in Kentish Town and would walk to Highbury for the games. He was an avid fan during the 1920s and 1930s, moving out of London to Soham in Cambridgeshire, where he turned on his radio to listen to his beloved Arsenal. He died some years ago so I can only guess his highs and lows. He would sit next to the tunnel and watch the team run out.

My grandad was sent cufflinks by Bertie Mee and the lads on his retirement. Grandad's reply is a fitting tribute to Arsenal, stating that if Arsenal became league champions, he would walk to London to congratulate them. That was 12th November 1970, the end of the season being 1971, the Double!

Maybe one day I will treasure a signed photograph of myself sitting, as my grandad always did, by the tunnel with Dennis Bergkamp or Tony Adams running out on to the pitch, as Eddie Hapgood did back then.

RIGHT

*Eddie Hapgood and Charlie
Jones (with the ball) run
out against Sheffield
Wednesday, both wearing
armbands in honour of
Herbert Chapman, who had
died that morning, 6th
January 1934. Both Henry
and Rubin Agent can be
seen in the crowd.*

C. J. PALFREY

The four-generation game

This is a short story of a family spanning four generations of Arsenal supporters, but mainly involving my father Mr C R Palfrey – born 1914, died 1997. My grandad saw Highbury being built in 1912, also seeing the first ever league game there. I remember my dad telling me he had a chance of buying some shares for £1.00 each but needed the money for deposit on their first house in Andover Road, about a mile from Highbury. In turn my Grandad took my Father to Highbury, standing at the "Laundry End" as it was then called [the North Bank originally abutted Mayfield's Laundry, situated just outside the ground]. My father saw Arsenal beat Sheffield Utd 1–0 in the 1936 FA Cup Final and went to Highbury as often as he could until the 1939–45 war.

My grandad died in 1956 when I was 7 years old, and I remember my father taking me to Arsenal v Wolves in 1958, standing in the North Bank behind Jack Kelsey's goal. I seem to remember three shillings [15p] as our turnstile payment.

My first decade came and went without a trophy in sight. We had to endure "that other North London club" winning the Cup and League.

But as we all know from 1970 until the present day we have more than made up for it.

Both my own sons aged 18 and 22 go to most home games, sharing with me our two North Bank Bond season tickets, so giving us our "four generations".

To finish my story I must say that I visited my father in Barnet Hospital after our 3–1 defeat by Blackburn on 13th December 1997. Although he was very ill, he gave a wry smile when I said "Dad, they were awful to-day. They won't win the League playing like that." Little did we know what lay ahead.

He died on 19th December 1997. Our very next game was away to Wimbledon, and we all know what happened in the first minute of the second half. Floodlight failure, match abandoned. It seemed so ironic and very strange.

The fact is that since my father's death Arsenal Football Club have not lost a Premier League game at home from 22nd December 1997 up to the day I am writing – 20th April 1999*. He would have been so proud.

*Arsenal's first home league defeat following this run was on 22nd August 1999 (1–2 to Manchester United)

ABOVE

The 1919 turnstile at the entrance to the West Stand.

RIGHT AND OPPOSITE

Sam Kinsey at work.

KEEPER OF THE GATE

"I had a trial for Arsenal once upon a time – I was bloody rubbish. In those days they had eight internationals in the reserves!"

That was in 1937. Sam Kinsey has been working on the turnstiles at Highbury since 1954, and by strange coincidence he is just a month older than the turnstile he works on, born in 1919.

"Been shut out twice in sixty- and seventy-thousand gates, so I told the Arsenal I could count money quicker than the blokes on the turnstiles. You see I worked in the British Rail treasury at the time. Only said it as a joke, that was 45 years ago."

Chatting to Sam you can almost touch and feel the memories of pre-war Arsenal, he has such an outgoing warmth and charm as he looks back to the

first glory years. He admits times have changed for him since he understudied Ted Drake. He enlightens the listener further: "I remember Alex James telling us – 'Ere laddie – football is played on the floor, not up in the air.' After he said that, I was rubbish".

Asked about Cliff Bastin, he shakes his head from side to side, "Oh dear, oh dear," face beaming. Raising one finger, wagging it in indignation, he says sternly: "You see I liked the pre-war football. They never crawled and fell over, obstructed people, never shammed this and that." And finally: "Never got injured."

TINA EVANS

The mother of all fans

My father, Tom Jales, has also written a note of his memories. Unfortunately he has been quite ill for some time and says he missed more games last season than the preceding seventy-eight years. As he has written, he is not in the photos, but my mum is – Rose Brinkman – and her father Albert (known as Patsy) Brinkman.

My mum told me many stories about her early life supporting the Arsenal. She was first taken by her father as a 5-year-old and in her teens became quite a mascot as it was unusual to see a woman so dressed up, indeed there were few women supporters then. She told me the teams were 'announced' by a little car going round on the cinder track around the pitch with someone holding up a board. She used to climb over the wall and hitch a lift, often taking with her Jimmy Clayton's duck! She was well known at Highbury and often had her picture in the Saturday evening papers.

She met my dad on an away train to Luton in 1934 when she was 18. I don't think my grandad would have let her marry anyone other than an Arsenal supporter. They married in 1938 in Islington, a short distance from Highbury. I was born in 1947 and my first memories are of getting the train from Harrow, up to Euston, bus or walk to Chapel Street, pie and mash in Maizies, then my nan would take me to my aunt's while my parents or grandad went to the Arsenal.

But on 26th November 1955 my grandparents took me to a jeweller's near Highbury Corner to buy me a ring for Christmas. After we got it I expected to go off with my nan to my aunt's but my grandad said I was going with him. We walked across Highbury Fields and I saw more and more people. Suddenly I knew where I was going, "I'm going to the Arsenal, aren't I, grandad?" I shouted. When I turned the corner at the top of Avenell Road I couldn't believe it, all these people, the air of excitement all around me. That feeling has never left me and even now although we have tickets in the West Stand I still walk all the way round every game just so I can turn that corner and look down Avenell Road. The Arsenal played Burnley that first time I went, I don't know what the score was [Arsenal 0 Burnley 1] but I still have the ticket and still wear the ring I got that day.

ABOVE
*Arsenal supporters leaving
St Pancras for Chesterfield
in the early morning, 16th
January 1937.*

Soon after that was the game against Manchester United just before the Munich tragedy. I had started to go to a few games and went to that one. Bearing in mind there was not the media coverage there is today, after Munich I remember being in school and crying because I had been there on Saturday and had seen those young men play. Other children couldn't understand me. I feel that was a privilege to have seen that match, even though we lost 5–4.

It is not a surprise that my children followed the family tradition in supporting Arsenal. But my husband took nearly thirty years to realise you can't beat us so you have to join us – he has a season ticket now. My son doesn't go to many games now but again it is up to the females in the family to carry on. My daughter is a real fanatic and has now converted her new husband.

For the Cup Final replay in 1993 Dawn was at college and had persuaded someone to drive her to the game whilst she used the driver's mirror to paint her face red and white. It was a rainy evening and the match was equally uninspiring. It looked like penalties and after sitting through nearly 240 minutes I couldn't face it. So I said to Dawn and my dad that I was going to hide in the ladies until it was all over. Dawn said "Wait a minute, mum, Merse is taking a corner". The rest, as they say, is history, Andy Linighan rose, headed, Chris Woods fumbled and it was in. There was a split second of shocked silence from both supporters until the red & white end erupted.

This letter was written by my mum Rose to her father while she was at a convalescent home in 1937. It shows how even the Arsenal players knew her. I always feel closest to her at Highbury as her ashes are buried in front of the North Bank, where she was first taken as a child.

Dear Dad

Thanks ever so much for both of your letters – you've no idea how something concerning football cheers me up. I hope Tom told you all about me running round after the Arsenal team, at last I saw them on the station as they were leaving on Sat morning. Alex James put the tin hat on it and asked me to kiss him. It ended in me going in their apartment in the train, kissing and wishing each one of them Good Luck.

G Allison was very interested in my welfare – wished me a lot better. Male was ever so jolly with me, said he had often wished to see me in civilian clothes for once instead of the old red and white. His wishes for my recovery in time for the Semi Final were quite sincere. Copping also nearly squeezed my hand to death. Eddie Hapgood promised me that they would win, if it was only for me, you can bet that I felt proud. Allison said the boys would be thinking of me while they were playing and he practically promised me two Cup Final tickets.

All that I daresay was just talk but even so it cheered me a lot and when I saw the result I kidded myself that they had won for me. No harm in that. Anyway I have written a letter of congratulations to them all – I feel like a close friend now.

I have read practically every report that I can. Thanks a lot for your papers, all the girls are quite thrilled about the whole affair and I have to sit and tell them of some of the games I have seen.

THOMAS J JALES

Ducks and Drake

The photograph of a crowd of us Arsenal supporters was taken in the 1930s. I am not in it, although I was there, the lady however was my wife –

unfortunately she passed away three years ago. She started to go to the Arsenal with her father when she was 5 years of age and was still going when she passed away at 79 years of age from a massive stroke. I myself am 86 years of age and still going. Fortunately my daughter and her husband, granddaughter and her husband take me and look after me.

BELOW
Rose on the shoulders of Albert Brinkman and Jimmy Clayton, without his duck! Arsenal beat Chesterfield 5–1 on that day in the FA Cup third round.

Way back in the 30s, we went everywhere to see them. One of our crowd was the chap who took a duck with us, his name was Jimmy Clayton. I started to go to Highbury when I was 8 years of age. So I have seen all the changes which all started with the arrival of Herbert Chapman. He built a great team – players who I saw were Moss, Male, Hapgood, Roberts, Copping, Grayston,

Hulme, Jack, Lambert, James, Bastin, Drake and several other fine players like Archie Macaulay, Forbes, Jones, Davidson and Bryn Jones. So I have seen them bring off two League and Cup Doubles and also the First Division championship three years running.

Obviously one of the most disappointing times was when Cardiff beat them 1–0 in the FA Cup in 1927, when Dan Lewis let the ball slip through his arms into the net. I could go on writing about all the great players I have seen play for Arsenal for ever, as well as players recently like Bergkamp, Petit, Vieira, Adams, Winterburn, Seaman and Overmars.

I will close on this note by just saying that I have seen some of the greatest players ever to kick the ball, and just as good as *Man Utd.*

* Thomas Jales died on 8th November 1999, and his ashes were laid next to Rose's at Highbury.

E DAVIS

The day we lost the War

Going back half a century and more to recall my first treasured memory of Arsenal FC. The occasion was the Wartime Cup Winners Final at Stamford Bridge, 15th May 1943. I was serving in the Royal Navy at the time and fortunate to be on weekend leave.

Living on the Isle of Anglesey but based in Portsmouth, it took me all day to travel by steam train home. So weekends were spent at the Welsh Service Club in Gray's Inn Road. Even then as a teenager I was completely hooked on the Gunners, and no wonder – they were still the all-conquering team and legendary side of the 30s.

The Final opponents were Blackpool, victorious in the League North Cup, beating Sheffield Wednesday. Our final of the League South Cup was played at Wembley on 1st May in front of 75,000. Arsenal thrashed Charlton 7–1, Reg Lewis contributing four goals, Drake two and Denis Compton completing the rout.

On Final day, Blackpool had borrowed players for the occasion, in fact more than half their team were guests. Their line-up: Savage (Queen of the South), Pope (Hearts), Hubbick (Bolton), Farrow, Hayward, Johnson, Stanley Matthews

ABOVE
Mr Davis in his 1930s replica shirt.

(Stoke, in his familiar No.7 shirt), Dix (Tottenham), Dodds, Finan, Burbanks (Sunderland). Arsenal had the availability of many pre-war staff, though during the war they had the highest losses of any club. Out of 42 professional players, they sadly lost nine.

The team that day was Marks, Scott, Leslie Compton, Crayston, Bernard Joy, Male, Kirchen, Drake, Lewis, Bastin and Denis Compton. To this day I can recall my intense excitement, in spite of the austere circumstances in war-torn London. Inside the ground, a large hole was observed on the terrace, the result of an unexploded bomb, presumably made safe or possibly removed. The match began sensationally in front of a crowd of over 55,000. Within six minutes of play Reg Lewis and Denis Compton had blasted the Gunners into a two-goal lead. Blackpool then gradually took control of the game, Dix and Burbanks saw them level the score by half-time. During the second half further goals from Dodds and Finan saw Blackpool attain a memorable victory, 4–2.

The result had been disappointing. However on leaving the ground and facing the tuppenny underground train journey back to King's Cross, I was both proud and happy. After all, hadn't I seen my heroes in action!

BRIAN SHARP

Two goals and a cough sweet

Happy memories are personal treasures. But in recording a few of mine, perhaps it will bring back memories for other people of the way things were at Arsenal. I wish I had a photograph of my first visit to Highbury. But I haven't, so I'll try and paint a picture for you.

The year is 1947. It's a warm, sunny September afternoon at the beginning of the second season after the war. Arsenal v Manchester United.

I'd been pestering my dad to take me to see the Gunners for some while, and he promised me that the first Saturday he didn't have to work, we would go.

My dad was a big Arsenal fan, and I'd been brought up on stories of the all-conquerinng pre-war teams when they had won seven trophies in nine years.

And about the greats of that era, like Alex James, Ted Drake and Cliff Bastin.

But now the great day has arrived. We get to the stadium very early. (You had to then. Only the elite had tickets.)

Already there are huge throngs of Arsenal supporters milling around the stadium.

And there's a fantastic air of anticipation and excitement. The buskers are coming up and down the queues. There's a one-man band; and a guy with no hair singing some old music hall song about his bald head and punctuating each verse by kicking himself on the head.

Inside, the stadium is busting with people. The atmosphere electric. And the North Bank so crammed, the kids who are at the top who can't see are being passed down to the front, over the heads of the colourful crowd. An amazing sight!

The minutes are ticking by to kick-off. It's 2.55pm. The police band and the baritone singer who used to entertain the crowd before the match in those days have finished and marched away. And suddenly a huge ear-splitting roar, as the 65,000 supporters greet the great Joe Mercer, as he leads out the Arsenal team. Absolute magic!

Inside the first twenty minutes, Ronnie Rooke, the Arsenal centre forward, receives the ball in the Manchester United half, midway between the halfway line and the penalty area. He moves to his right, looks up and fires a shot that travels like a rocket into the top left hand corner of United's goal. Crompton, the United keeper, can only clutch at the air. Rooke, as though he knows it's going to hit the back of the net, actually turns and walks back to the centre spot before the ball hits its target.

The final score: Arsenal 2 Manchester 0. And the Gunners go on to win their sixth League Championship.

During the match there must have been someone close to us who was sucking cough sweets. To this day, if I catch even a whiff of a cough sweet, I'm transported back fifty years and I'm standing on the terraces at Highbury watching my very first match… and Arsenal are beating Manchester United two–nil.

Eighty years after my dad first set foot in what was then the new Arsenal Stadium, I took my grandchildren, both Junior Gunners, to their first match. How will they remember it in fifty years time? What will trigger their memories? It could have been my imagination, but was there someone close to us sucking cough sweets?

LESLIE STONE

First of the flying Gooners

The 1949–50 season was the first in which organised groups of Arsenal supporters travelled to away games. The occasion was the founding of the Arsenal Supporters Club by R.B. Jones, a former RAF officer. His driving force made it possible. After several unsuccessful attempts to convince the board of directors to give the project their blessing – they evidently feared that it would try to undermine their authority in all kinds of ways – Jones proceeded to call an eve-of-the-season public meeting at the old Odeon cinema in Upper Street, close to Islington Town Hall.

Having received an enthusiastic vote of endorsement from the audience of about 200 people, he called for volunteers to join a committee to establish the club. I, now a fifteen-year-old schoolboy, pushed my father forward. Born in Clerkenwell, he had been an Arsenal supporter since the move to Highbury. He took me to my first reserve game in 1938 – the days of Alex Wilson, George Marks, Alf Fields, Ernie Collett, the Compton brothers and the great Reg Lewis, who would surely have shattered all Arsenal goal scoring records but for Adolf Hitler and subsequent knee injuries.

I saw the 1941 and 1943 Cup Finals at Wembley and the sad defeat by Blackpool at Stamford Bridge in the North v South Cup-Winners play-off. The 679 trolley bus from Smithfield to White Hart Lane took me regularly to wartime home games. I was at the 6–0 FA defeat at the hands of West Ham in 1946 and the first post-war home match at bomb-battered Highbury – a 3–1 loss to Blackburn, who had the newly transferred George Marks in goal.

However, 1949 was the first time we came in regular contact with other Arsenal fanatics, apart that is from the small group around us who stood in the same place at the Clock End for every home game. The Supporters Club brought hitherto strangers together. When five of us went by car to Huddersfield in early September, we felt like true pioneers. Because there were no motorways, we made an early start from the Angel, at the top of the City Road, before the bus or tube had come alive. Nevertheless, we didn't get to our destination till shortly before kick-off. (Helpful Huddersfield people had directed us first to the Rugby League ground.) Then, once inside the stadium, we wondered whether we had been wise to come. The crowd was small, only 20,000 or so. Bedecked in red-and-white scarves and rosettes, we stood out – the only Arsenal supporters visible in what was from the outset a very hostile environment.

Arsenal had made a miserable start to the season – four defeats in the first six games – and it seemed things would get worse. Ronnie Burke, a recent high-priced signing from Manchester United, scored twice for Huddersfield. But chasing a long through ball he collided with the out-rushing George Swindin and was carried off with a bad knee injury. A goal for Arsenal was greeted with grim silence. With ten-man Huddersfield holding on and Arsenal playing poorly, Eddie Boot, a veteran of the 1938 Cup Final, twisted his ankle with no-one within yards of him, and became a limping passenger on the left wing.

Thereafter, every Arsenal tackle was deemed illegal, a premeditated crime, by the baying mob. We cautiously moved away into an isolated pocket of seats – there was plenty of empty space in the stand – as looks became more threatening. Then, with a minute or two left, Peter Goring scored to make it 2–2. The Huddersfield fury off the pitch knew no bounds. It was a foul, hands, offside! Then the final whistle blew. Those lucky, dirty Londoners had escaped their just fate. The booing continued till the players left the field.

We could not afford to wait that long and walked quickly to our car, clambering into it with a sense of relief. But the getaway was not to be that easy. Slowly moving down the street through the homeward-bound Huddersfield fans, we were soon spotted wearing our Arsenal scarves. Fists were raised, insults hurled, doors and windows banged. More ominously they began to rock the car. Only the determination of the driver, keeping his head up and his foot down, saw us through the gathering mass of bodies. For a moment things had seemed out of control. We were very glad to escape from Huddersfield unscathed.

Not that our troubles were over. We had been warned before starting out that the car was a bit temperamental. Perhaps the rocking had unsettled it. Certainly by the time we reached Sheffield we knew all was not well. But we snatched some food while a mechanic looked the vehicle over and we were soon limping back to London. Unfortunately, when we got to Stamford in

Lincolnshire on the A1, it packed up completely. We were stuck, at 10 o'clock on a Saturday night, miles away from home. No buses, no trains, no hotel room. We decided to sleep in the car. Miraculously, a saviour then turned up, pulling into the garage for a petrol refill. It took the form of a London cab with a happy punter – or was it a bookmaker? – inside. He was coming back with his winnings from the St Leger at Doncaster in a very good mood. Generously he offered us a lift. We all piled in and were back at the Angel in the early hours. It had been quite a day.

Further trips to games that season went more smoothly, but were by today's standards still unusual. On Boxing Day 1949 Arsenal supporters composed the first organised group to fly to a league game in England. It was R.B. Jones's idea. How else could we get to Old Trafford on Monday and back for the return fixture at Highbury the next day, when there was no public transport? Obviously we had to go by plane. After all, the team were doing well. Following that draw at Huddersfield, they had gone on a long successful run with only one more defeat till mid-December. We had to be there. So a party of 20 or so clambered aboard an old Dakota belonging to a small private airline early on Boxing Day morning and flew to Manchester. We took heed of advice and soon began to swallow hard, and were still swallowing ten minutes later. The unfortunate part was that we still had not left the ground. The plane was still warming up its engines before heading for the runway.

Our party became airborne at 10.20am and after a smooth trip over the Midlands touched down at Ringway Airport, Manchester, at noon, where a coach was waiting to take us to the ground. We stood in small groups scattered around Old Trafford and watched Arsenal go down 2–0. The mood on the plane afterwards was rather sombre. Tea was taken at the airport restaurant before we took off at 5.45pm, with the nose of the aircraft headed for the south and home. But the battle was not quite over for us air-minded supporters. By now, in our opinion, experienced fliers, we viewed the return leg with supreme confidence. This was a major mistake, for at least three of the party succumbed to air-sickness before we finally touched down at Stansted. The pilot said that he had been trying to get out of the wind, which explained our constant change in height. But we felt we were setting a precedent, starting a trend, pioneers again.

A few days later, at 10 o'clock on Friday night, another band of supporters, about thirty in all, boarded a coach outside Arsenal Stadium bound for Liverpool. Again with no motorways, such a trip took eight to ten hours. It was around 6am on 31st December that we disembarked at Lime Street Station and headed for the wash-and-brush-up facilities, clutching our toilet and shaving equipment. That game too was lost 2–0, effectively ending our championship hopes. Wearily dropping off for refreshments at a roadside café en route home, it was a strange way to see in the New Year.

But, of course, it was all to end in triumph. One week into 1950 Reg Lewis scored a late winner against Sheffield Wednesday to give Arsenal only their second FA Cup tie victory since the war. Swansea were defeated in a turbulent fourth-round tie, and next came Burnley, at that time a major force to be reckoned with. It was decided that the game must be all-ticket, the first at Highbury I believe, and I simply had to be there.

The problem was that I was still at boarding school in Sussex. Discipline was strict. No one was permitted to venture beyond the school boundaries without permission, even when accompanied by parents, and boys were forbidden to enter any public place such as a cinema or theatre during term time, lest they import a nasty, contagious disease. Besides, we wore sixteenth-century uniform – a long, dark blue cassock-like garment with its skirt stretching down to the ankles, clerical bands, knee breeches and yellow stockings. It was quite something to wear this travelling from home to inner-London to Victoria station and the special train to school. Heads would turn. Onlookers would snigger.

Obviously, going to Highbury in such a garb was impossible. Who knows, one might be photographed, it might get into the papers. I was not supposed to be there. Clearly special measures were called for. I don't know what excuses I gave or how I managed to catch the London train. I probably just bunked off. But I do remember my mother coming to meet me at Victoria with a ticket for the match and a suitcase packed with a change of clothes. I changed in the gents, deposited the case with my school uniform in left luggage, and set off on the tube, getting to Highbury minutes before kick-off. It was raining, there were puddles and the touts outside the station still had bundles of tickets in their hands. Although the match was officially sold out, attendance was a mere 55,000 – receipts a magnificent £8,058 – a few thousand lower than the Swansea tie.

I stood in the East Stand enclosure on the North Bank side of the halfway line and had a good view of both goals. Reg Lewis scored with a typical shot from the edge of the penalty area. Denis Compton, recently recalled to the side, hit a fierce left-footer into the net before wheeling away in delight. I returned to school walking on air.

I couldn't get to the sixth-round game versus Leeds and the young John Charles, or either of the semi-finals against Chelsea. The risk was too great. The BBC broadcast only the second half of matches. But I recall the radio commentator beginning the transmission of the first Chelsea semi-final –

against a very noisy background, "You come to us at a moment of great drama. Arsenal have just scored a most extraordinary goal, direct from a corner taken by Cox... however, they still trail two–one." Happily, Leslie Compton equalised, Freddie Cox scored a famous replay winner and Arsenal were in the Final.

Getting tickets for Wembley was much more difficult than today. The finalists were restricted to about 10,000 each. Arsenal had an average gate in the region of 50,000. After season ticket-holders had been accounted for, there were precious few left for those on the terraces. In our case I think R.B. Jones was crucial. The directors had come to realise early on that he was indeed a help not a hindrance. The Supporters Club despatched a small fleet of coaches from Avenell Road to Wembley. We were handed signs, and rattles with which to demonstrate our presence. I was given a bell, painted in gold, the Arsenal shirt colours for the day. (Both sides had to change, Liverpool won the toss for second colours and played in white.) Again, it poured. The high terraces behind both goals were uncovered. The paint on my bell was fresh and it began to run, spreading over my raincoat. I did not care. Reg Lewis scored a beauty from a Jimmy Logie pass right in front of us. Then he got another from a Freddie Cox back-heel at the other end.

We were delirious. Joe Mercer clutched the Cup. We chanted for him to bring it down to our end, but he went straight to the dressing rooms in the distance. On the journey back to Highbury we hung out of the coaches, ringing bells and whirling rattles. That night my father and I went to see the Harringay Racers play ice hockey, still wearing our Arsenal rosettes. It was a decorous celebration but people kept coming up between periods, offering drinks and asking what it had been like to actually be at Wembley.

The Double was over twenty years off, when my own son would be standing beside me, witnessing another Final triumph over Liverpool.

STUART JARMAN

Forever Arsenal

The photograph I enclose was taken in September 1995 and was a very sad day but a special day, for it was when the ashes of my father – Frederick John Jarman, were buried in the North Bank goalmouth. My father was 73 when he died on 8th May 1995, and had supported Arsenal from the 1930s. He often recalled memories about the days of Bastin, Jack, James and company. My mum and dad married in December 1947 and a month later dad took her to Highbury for an FA Cup tie against Bradford. Arsenal became champions that season, but on that particular day in a shock result Bradford triumphed 1–0. Needless to say, few words were said on the way home. My mum was branded a jinx and was not to go to Highbury for another 49 years. Dad was very superstitious and in later years, when we had not gone to the match, my mum was not allowed in the same room when we were listening to the radio.

My sister was born in 1950 the day after we defeated Liverpool in the Cup Final and it wasn't long before she was taken to Highbury – we must have won for she was allowed to go again. I was born in 1965 and one of my first memories concerned a week in May 1971. We were living in Lewisham at the time and my father was in hospital with pneumonia. On the Monday the door bell rang, we were surprised to see my father, who had discharged himself from hospital in order to listen to the Tottenham match at White Hart Lane. Of course we won, thanks to Ray Kennedy, and completed the first leg of the double.

A couple of days later my father was released from hospital and so was at home to watch the Cup Final on television. I remember being in tears when Steve Heighway gave Liverpool the lead and going to sit on the stairs. My father came out and consoled me saying that we would win, we went back into the living room and half an hour later we were all celebrating Arsenal's first Double.

I was now a regular spectator along with my father. Another match that brings back memories was the Arsenal v Wolves match at Highbury in 1976. Arsenal were going through a transitional period and were still in fear of relegation, and with the game tied at 1–1 the crowd erupted when the bald

ABOVE
Steve Braddock, the Highbury groundsman (left), with the Jarman family at the ceremony in the North Bank goalmouth.

BELOW
Frank and his sister outside their flat in the late 1940s with the East Stand behind them.

head of Terry Mancini rose to head the winning goal. Arsenal did not win again that season, but escaped the drop. Wolves were relegated.

I remember awaiting the train at Euston for the 1979 FA Cup semi-final versus Wolves at Villa Park and having the late Bobby Moore standing just behind us saying that he thought Arsenal should win. The FA Cup win over Manchester United was another memorable day. I can quite vividly recall the pounding of feet on the terraces and the thought that someone was going to be hurt seriously when Alan Sunderland scored the winning goal.

Of course in more recent years there have been many more memorable experiences, George Graham's League Cup in 1987 after eight years without a trophy, Anfield in 1989. One defeat in the league in '90–91, the Double Cup win in '93. Copenhagen in '94 and the 1998 Double under Arsène Wenger. Hopefully there will be many more highs to come. I really am glad my father had Arsenal blood in him. Can you imagine how happy he would be, laid to rest at Highbury. By the way, I took my mum to Highbury in 1996 for the match against Coventry. We still didn't win (1–1) and Ian Wright missed a penalty, so she still hasn't got rid of her jinx tag.

There have been many great players, and many memorable matches that my family have seen over the years and hopefully will continue to do so, as we have Arsenal in our veins.

FRANK HUMMELL

No place like home

I was born in Avenell Mansions right next to the Stadium and my family had been supporting Arsenal since 1913 when we moved to Highbury from Woolwich.

Therefore I have witnessed the whole ground being built from the Thirties to the present day, and I knew Kenny Friar when he kicked a ball around in Avenell Road.

At the outbreak of the Second World War in September 1939 I was a small boy of eight, living in the shadow of the East Stand, not being allowed to attend matches, apart from the odd reserve game, due to the large crowds. So I was more than happy to collect cigarette cards from the many discarded cigarette packets in the empty streets surrounding the ground.

From where I lived in the rear block of Avenell Mansions you couldn't see into the Arsenal football ground. However, a bomb dropped during the Blitz in 1941, and it landed on the corner of the Clock End demolishing the "cottage" and the houses opposite thus creating a view which we did not have before.

In the early Fifties we used to travel all over the country with the supporters club. I met my wife Jessie on one of those trips. We have been married for forty-three years and my son and I are bondholders in the North Bank. So far I have five grandchildren, all of which are Junior Gunners.

Back in 1954 I was in Switzerland with the Arsenal Supporters Club for the World Cup. We all dressed in smart blazers with the Club Badge proudly displayed.

LEFT
*Sunderland v Arsenal.
Travelling away in the
snows of winter,
3rd January 1953.*

On the way by coach to the third place decider between Uruguay and Austria we were delayed in traffic. Arriving at the ground the standing terraces where we had tickets were packed and we could not get in. I thought, "Gosh, we have come all this way and we are not even going to see the match". Then I suddenly thought, "How good is Arsenal's name?" I managed to find a steward and unable to speak his language just pointed to the badge on my blazer. With that, just like magic we were immediately escorted along the touchline and allowed to sit on the ground at the halfway line next to the players' dugout.

TOMMY ROOKS

The boy at the front of the queue

At the end of World War Two my father, back from the army and an Arsenal supporter for many years, thought it was time for me to become a supporter. So in 1946/47 aged 13 my Arsenal life started, and I am still at Highbury aged 66. Having a season ticket in East Upper A for over 35 years and a supporter for 53 years, my memories are many. How do I start?

My first memory – 8th January 1949. Arsenal v Spurs FA Cup, queued all night just to get front seat on the rail East Lower. This is how it was reported in the press at that time:

A chubby-faced fifteen-year-old boy wearing a red and white top hat, a red jacket and white trousers, and a red tie with the word "Arsenal" painted on it in white, arrived outside Highbury at 6 o'clock last night. Tommy Rooks – self-styled Arsenal mascot – was the first in the queue for the 9,000 unreserved seats for the first ever Arsenal v Tottenham cup-tie match.

Although he had a wait of twenty hours before him, Tommy was happy. "Joe Mercer – the Arsenal captain – has promised to introduce me to both teams tomorrow," he said. "And I'm going to parade around the ground before the match."

He had with him a ply-wood replica of the FA Cup. "I've given this match a lot of thought and I'm sure my team will win," he said.

Armed with blankets, thermos flasks and food satchels, supporters of both teams settled down for the night. Many of them keeping warm by waving rattles, ringing bells – and in one case by blowing a bugle.

We won 3–0 but did not make the final.

LEFT
Tommy Rooks ringing his bell at the 1950 Cup Final.

STEP
INSIDE

ABOVE

The view from the Clock End.

PERFECT PITCH

Arsenal's award-winning groundsman Steve Braddock is in constant pursuit of perfection, but his is not the usual fruitless search for this football Holy Grail – he continually delivers.

Since coming from the university sports ground at The Royal Veterinary College twelve years ago, he has won the Groundsman of the Year accolade an astonishing five times. "It gets a bit embarrassing now. I have just won it two years on the trot, which has never been done before, something I didn't think I would ever be able to do – but I have. I'm quite chuffed with that."

You would think Steve would feel proud when the team runs out all over his work at the start of the season – but not so... "I always find that the most tense time, because you don't know from one season to the next how

your pitch is going to perform. If there are loads of divots coming out after the first couple of games then you know you're going to be in for a lot of trouble. The tension that's involved supersedes the feeling of pride. I'm just thinking… have I put enough water on it? Is the grass growing too long? Is the surface going to be too hard? Is it too soft?"

Before the match it is important that he checks the pitch to make sure there is nothing on it, no "unwanted enemies" as he puts it. "It could be anything – a sharp stone, a sliver of glass, you name it. When you have £10million players running around, it needs to be safe. You don't want anything out there that could injure a player."

He has only one assistant – Paul Burgess – and you can sense the intensity as they work together to make that Perfect Pitch.

Steve has a problem with "match day pigeons", the ones that for some reason visit only on match days and leave little feathers all over the pitch. He parades birds of prey around the ground sometimes as a deterrent but the pigeons still turn up. "It's as if they know it's match day, but the thing is you never actually see the birds, just their feathers. It's strange."

Does the team ever comment on the playing surface? "Only when they feel there is something wrong with it – I suppose it depends if they win 6–0 or not. But I've been here twelve years and just about know what the players want, and it's down to me to give it to them. You are going to get times when they are going to complain, 'The grass is too long, Steve' – when I know it's not – but you can't please everybody all the time."

During the close season the pitch undergoes a process of 'renovation'. This is a fascinating procedure and in many ways really tells the story, and perhaps the secret, of how Highbury continues to have the best playing surface in the Premiership.

It begins with a process of scarifying, which removes all the unwanted vegetation from the pitch. This leaves the pitch more receptive to drainage material – like sand. Next is a process called "hollow tining" – a machine takes up cores of soil, which leave a hole five inches in depth from the surface, with the cores left on top – then they're broken up and worked back into the surface.

Following that, a dressing of 40 tons of sand is spread on to the pitch, followed by a further hollow tining. So yet more holes appear, and the soil that is in the pitch is mixed with the sand, and once again worked back in to the holes. Then you are left with a till ready for seeding in three or four directions. After the seeding process, a Verti-Drain machine puts holes measuring ten inches deep

and three-quarters of an inch in diameter into the pitch. Now it's ready for the next dressing – kiln-dried sand spread by hand over the entire pitch and brushed into the Verti-Drain holes. All these processes allow an improvement in the drainage system for the coming season.

"Once this job is completed, there is a chance you could have disturbed the seed you have already laid, so the pitch is gone over again in three or four different directions, with even more seed."

What Steve would like is all the drainage work first and the seeding job last,

but because he faces ever-increasing problems in the amount of time he has to establish the grass, the seed has to go on a little bit earlier. The renovation process takes three to four weeks. "The sooner you can get the seed in, the more time it has to establish itself and develop, before the first game of the season."

Germination sheets are then placed over the pitch, to stop the birds from having a feast and also, acting as a greenhouse, to influence the germination of the seed. The sheets keep the heat and dampness in – plenty of moisture is needed for a seed to sprout.

The seeds are Perennial Rye grass – from Holland, where else? "But it's not about the grass, it's the drainage that is the important factor," says Steve. "There is too much emphasis on the product on the top, it's what is underneath that is the real secret!"

It was not always like this, with pitches good enough for bowling on, let alone playing football. Steve remembers well… "If you look at the pitches in the Eighties they were all dire. The improvement is due to a revolution in pitch maintenance, there is a lot more technology available now. Since the arrival of Sky TV, clubs tend to take a bit more care of the pitch, whereas years ago, it was accepted that if you had grass down the middle by December it was something

exceptional. Things have completely changed – if you don't have any grass around
the centre circle by December people want to know why".

However, this problem has resurfaced again at certain grounds. "Can you name
one good pitch in the league in a closed-in stadium that doesn't have to be re-
turfed in mid-season? There isn't one. If only architects would listen to
groundsmen, you wouldn't have the big clubs digging up their pitches so often.
We have a vicious circle, with the price of seats and punters demanding a roof

RIGHT

Line-painting before the match, viewed from the North Bank roof.

ABOVE

Steve draws the line.

RIGHT

Steve marking out the lines, ready for painting.

over their heads. They don't want to get wet, so the architects provide the roof. But the pitch suffers. Most teams today like to play the ball on the floor, and with a bad surface you are not going to see a good game of football."

The way a stadium can mould a playing surface can be clearly seen at Highbury. In the Eighties the camber on the pitch from the middle to the wings was as much as 40.5 to 61 centimetres (16 to 24 inches). Today it is only about 20 centimetres (eight inches). The reason is to aid natural drainage – most of the playing activity during a game is through the middle, and if you can encourage the water to move on to the wings, then it will help. Also, the pitch is graded down to the supporters' seats. Look at the North Bank – there is a tremendous slope-off from the goal line to the seats to help their view of the game. Over time, with all the renovations, a little more soil is added each year, and if the pitch surface was brought up to the level of

the centre circle it would create a huge step up from the outside track. So it's all graded down to suit the contours of the stadium and keep the supporter happy.

When you see the pitch being prepared and nurtured by Steve and Paul it is easy to understand why they don't want many people walking on it. Steve has a very strict policy on that.

"No-one... *no-one* is supposed to walk on the pitch – so why are referees and guests allowed on there? Well – if I had the choice I wouldn't let them." He smiles. "If it was down to me, you wouldn't have any activities at all before the game on the pitch. It's just unnecessary wear and tear. I am in this game to produce the best surface for the players to play on. I believe any activities before the game have a detrimental effect on the pitch. They just add to traffic on the surface, and the more traffic, the worse the pitch will get as the season continues.

"The problem is, because the club is successful it puts more pressure on you. All you are thinking about is, if the club wins the league on the pitch – on, say, the last game of the season – what's everyone going to do? They're going to run all over it, aren't they, they are going to damage what you have done, and that damage could be irreparable." A sobering thought, and one that illustrates just how delicate that award-winning pitch is.

LEFT

Walking the pitch before the game.

Pat O'Connor, Highbury ground electrician since February 1965, and Arthur Young, plumber at Highbury since December 1969. Before every game their "office" deep under the West Stand becomes a focal point for the stewards and staff as they gather to discuss Arsenal's tactics.

ABOVE AND LEFT
A new signing arrives at Highbury.

A GUNNER KEEPING THE POWDER DRY

For the supporters at home, washing one or two replica Arsenal shirts after a game is a warming experience, especially if it follows a victory. Things are not so different in the laundry room high above the East Stand – except Jean Scorey, the laundry mistress, washes up to 400 shirts a week.

Each player has two home, two away and two Champions League shirts. He might well also have non-Premiership shirts and a Charity Shield set. And for every match he will have two long-sleeve and two short-sleeve shirts in the kit bag. Although these obviously don't all need washing every week, the average Arsenal laundry bag is bolstered with shirts from many other players – the Reserves, for example, the Youth team, the Schoolboys and the highly successful Ladies team.

A visit to Jean even on a normal working-load day guarantees the sound of the washing machines' constant rumbling, keeping up with the tide of red, white and yellow shirts littering the floor in baskets. The sight is overwhelming – as if you had invited every Gooner you had ever met for a kickabout in the park and then asked your poor mum to take care of the shirts.

Jean and her assistant Julie Coxall sit in a corner engulfed by the heat of the dryers. "You see we wash everything, including all the undergarments – and I even do ironing for the staff, when they need it. We scrub

BELOW

The away kit packed.

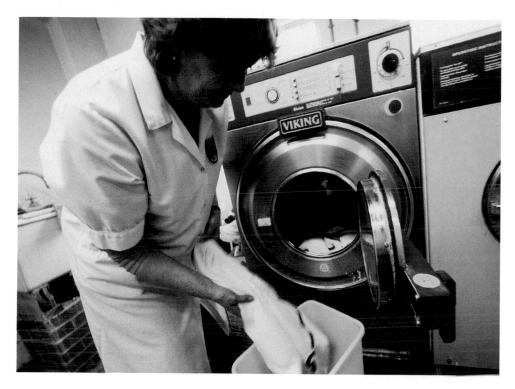

all the players' shirts by hand first, working on all the collars and dirty marks, then we just put them into the washing machine on a warm wash."

In a side drying room away from the whirling machines lies a quiet inner sanctum – here only the first team shirts hang, drying on the original 1930s heating pipes.

Does any of this famous kit go missing? "Oh yeah, players give away kits – goalkeepers the most, so then we have to get a replacement done. I have a name printer handy, for the really quick jobs. But it's not all work, we do have some laughs too, especially when the kit is mixed up. You've got the big players trying to get into large when they are all XXL, now that is funny. They sort of stand there and can't get them above their knees, the slip pants more than the shorts!"

Who is the dirtiest player, the one who comes in at full-time with a shirt that needs special treatment? Without hesitation, "No. 4 and No. 17 are very good in the tackles – they will slide along on the pitch, Petit and Vieira 'sliding tackles' we call them. I'm on duty during all home games, I get to see the game as I sit in the paddock, so if anything is needed I am available. I even come up here at half time and start washing. If it's Sunday and there is packing to be done on a Monday for a journey to a match on a Tuesday, I will stay on to midnight to get it done. We don't operate a seven-day working week, it's more like eight."

After working at Highbury for over seventeen years Jean has experienced many special moments. "When we won the Double in '98 – after all the hard work which the team and myself had put in, I was very proud of all of the boys."

She can sometimes be seen before the game looking out of the laundry window, high above the changing rooms, glancing at the supporters down below. "When I am up here working, I hear the team arrive and the roar goes up – the goosebumps still appear. The day they don't, or the day when I turn the corner to the ground and I don't get a lovely feelin' – then that will be it."

BELOW AND OPPOSITE

The inner shirt sanctum.

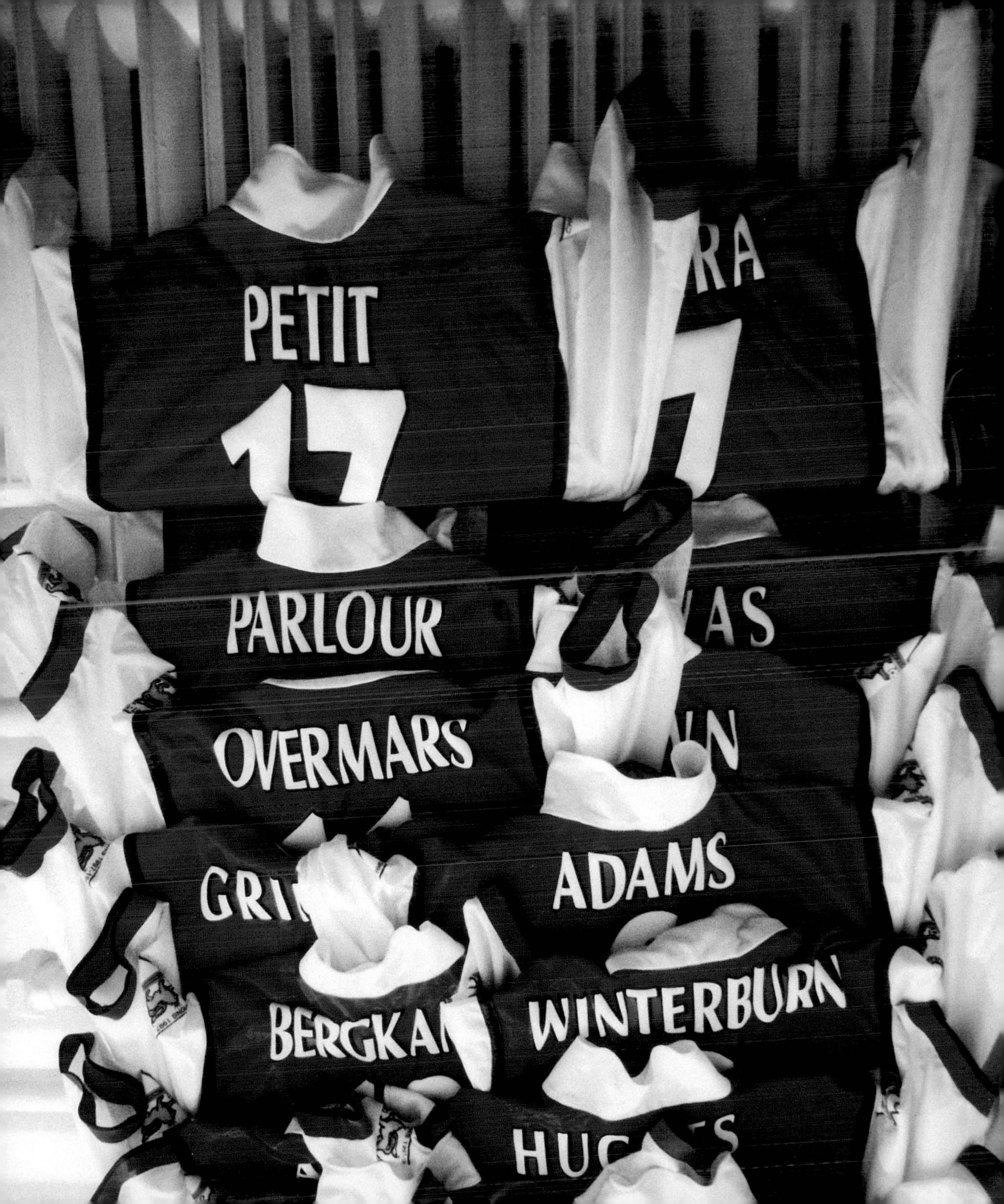
PETIT
17
PARLOUR
OVERMARS
ADAMS
WINTERBURN

THE POST-WAR YEARS

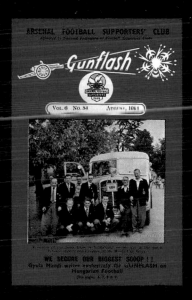

G. L. WILLIAMS

The non-playing captain

In the summer of 1949 my brother and I took a holiday at the Devon Coast Country Club (a fancy name for a posh holiday camp). Through our mutual love of football we became friendly with a Mr Taylor and his wife, who came from Liverpool. When we had a kickabout he claimed he was not allowed to take part. The next May we knew why, when we saw Phil Taylor captain Liverpool at Wembley in the 1950 Cup Final. We were behind the goal where Reg Lewis scored and Phil Taylor was injured.

Now in my eightieth year, I have supported the Gunners since the Chapman era. A season ticket holder since army demob in the 1940s, I have always lived within walking distance of the stadium and still do the walk to and fro today. I have fond memories of those early days; I remember that floodlit game against Glasgow Rangers. I recall a full house once for a reserve game when Tommy Lawton played for Chelsea second team, and what a splendid game Alf Fields had against him.

The old greats that introduced me to the club have a special place in my heart. I could name them all, and often wonder how they would have performed in today's hurly-burly. There can't be many left now who saw Cliff Bastin create the goal-scoring record so recently broken by Ian Wright.

After 70 years of highs and lows, I no longer kick the cat if we lose! I may add that since the war I have attended every Wembley match the club has been involved in. You can see that once I start I don't know when to stop – please excuse. Wishing my club continued success.

JAMES WEBB

Clock End delivery

I was first taken to Highbury on the odd occasion around 1936, about the time Alf Fields started. My most vivid memory before the war was after we beat Bolton 5–0 and won the title in 1938. My dad lifted me over the railings, North-West corner, followed me over and tried to nick the corner flag as a souvenir. Someone beat him to it and he moaned for days afterwards.

Got demobbed in June 1949. Met my wife a week later. Introduced her to the Arsenal on August 20th v Burnley (lost 0–1). This coming August Evelyn celebrates her fifty years in the East Stand. Her favourite now is Patrick Vieira. Used to be Alex Forbes and George Armstrong.

Her only claim to fame was that she danced with Jim Fotheringham at the supporters club dance at the Seymour Hall Baths, Paddington, in 1954. Eve also managed to dance with Jimmy Logie who was more of her size. I can claim to have had a few words with Brian Clough in the City Ground car park (nothing too offensive) after our youth team had beaten Notts Forest 3–0 in the semi-final of Youth Cup in April 1988. Pat Rice would confirm that.

My only memorable claim to fame was on 18th March 1950 at White Hart Lane in the semi-final v Chelsea. Due to overcrowding we were allowed to sit on the grass verge behind the goalmouth. My idol Les Compton scored the equaliser where we sat. I ran onto the field and caught up with him on the half-way line. I can't repeat what he said to me! The referee had a few words as well. I returned to my spot with Eve behind the goal for the last ten minutes. I have often wondered if the incident was ever recorded on Movietone News.

My son was born in 1957, and was named Leslie…

My daughter was born at the Royal Northern, Holloway Road. She as a small claim to fame inasmuch as she was carried out of the ground before she was born. My wife and I were at the Clock End due to ticket allocation in November 1954. We were playing Spartak Moscow in a friendly. Due to crowd pressure she passed out after twenty minutes, and was helped off the terraces hand over head to the railings and was carried on a stretcher into the East Stand. The doctor who attended her told me off. So I said to him: "You try keeping her away".

My daughter arrived three months later, and her favourite player is Ray Parlour.

We now have a granddaughter named Vivienne Louise who is eighteen months old and was a registered Junior Gunner within a week of being born.

I would just like to add a note to accompany the photograph taken in Woolworth's cafeteria in 1951. In those days when you travelled up North it was always an overnight job. You would leave Highbury Corner at approximately 8 o'clock on the Friday night.

My wife and I have spent our life together following the Arsenal. The first team, also the youth team and for a few seasons the Ladies football team. I am sure if it were possible we would both do it all over again.

"Up the Gunners."

GEOFFREY GILBERT

Ten men against the odds

At the moment the final whistle went at Wembley to signal Arsenal's Cup win over the Magpies my mind was back to 1952, when under a grey sky a valiant and magnificent Arsenal side down to ten men after twenty minutes lost 1–0 in the Cup Final to Newcastle. I looked round the stadium with its seething mass of colour and realised that there were possibly only a few hundred or so Arsenal fans who were still left to be at Wembley for this moment of triumph.

On the Saturday in question in 1952 I was stationed at RAF Honington in Suffolk, and having been unable to obtain a 48-hour pass I had to be content with a 36. That meant that the coach to London which left at midday had to run smoothly to get me to Manor House tube by 2.00pm at the latest. It did. I arrived at Wembley at 3.10, which was really remarkable.

Ten minutes after my arrival Walley Barnes, a wonderful two-footed full-back, suffered an injury which was to badly affect his career and make Arsenal's "Lucky" tag seem rather incongruous; especially when you consider we had been chasing the Double that season, but over the Easter period had suffered a succession of injuries which seemed more like a jinx. We also had Lishman and Logie in the side, who had come out of hospital only a few days earlier. No substitutes in those days.

From this moment on the Arsenal, down to ten men, were forced to rearrange their team with Roper going to full-back, and the battle was on.

Remember on that big Wembley pitch it was a handicap. This is when the Arsenal showed why they were and always have been a team who are at their best when the fates conspire against them.

They still tried to take the game to Newcastle, at one stage the ball rolling all along the Newcastle bar with everyone waiting for it to drop in – but no, it went out for a goal kick.

Joe Mercer, in my opinion Arsenal's greatest captain (then in his mid-thirties), was covering every blade of grass shouting, geeing up and inspiring his defenders; tackling and trying to push back the wave of Newcastle attacks in the second half. It was an inspiring performance. But in the end the team, some of whom were not 100 per cent fit, gradually began to tire. And then with about seven minutes to go Robledo scored the decisive goal.

So a season which had promised so much produced nothing. Yet as an Arsenal supporter I left Wembley sad but proud of a fighting display which epitomised the Arsenal and all that they stand for, and a captain's display by Joe Mercer which I remember to this day. Your team does not always have to win for you to be proud of them. So when Tony Adams lifted that Cup in May I felt the team of 1952 had been honoured as well.

BILL MANSER

The day they played in all-white

The photograph was taken at Horsmonden in Kent, and it features players from Arsenal and a local cricket side. These games were an annual event in the Fifties and Sixties and were usually played in late August or early September. I played for a club in Tonbridge, but I worked with one of the Horsmonden team and in 1958 I was invited by him to play in the game, which was for me, as a life-long supporter, a great honour. It was, as far as I can remember, a low-scoring affair with Arsenal scoring around 110 and Horsmonden just winning by two wickets. The Arsenal players there that day: Cliff Holton, Gordon Nutt, Derek Tapscott, Don Bennett, Jack Kelsey, Leslie Compton, Peter Goy, Jim Standen, Stan Charlton, Tony Briggs, Bill Dodgin, Roy Gordon and Ray Swallow.

My wife was unable to attend the game as she was heavily pregnant with our daughter at the time. She was extremely pleased when the photograph was taken because I was standing on the left of our hero, Leslie Compton. On the birth of our daughter at the end of September we named her Lesley after the man himself.

Now in my seventy-fourth year, I am so proud that she takes her son regularly to watch the Arsenal, as they are both mad Gooners.

PETER LEVINGHAM

Like father, like son

My first Arsenal match was on 25th April 1959, a 5–2 win over relegation-bound Portsmouth. I was seven years old. I recall little or nothing about the game, except the bright orange colour of the ball, the incredible noise when a goal was scored and the Portsmouth goalkeeper being stretchered off. My father told me to look out for the heroes of the day, Jack Kelsey and David Herd (neither of whom apparently played).

Nearly thirty years later I took my son Alexander to his first game. We played Portsmouth on their return to the First Division. Four-year-old Alex, dressed in his replica kit, emerged from the stairs in the West Stand and asked me how we were going to get down to the pitch and why we had not brought our football from home. After Arsenal had scored four in what was a 6–0 win, there was a lull in the scoring. It was at this point that Alex announced that it was time to go home as the match was boring without goals.

Alex and I now attend most Arsenal matches home and away.

There is something very special about Highbury – which I defy anyone to truly explain. Perhaps it is the small pitch and the

ABOVE
Arsenal in their cricket whites.

BELOW
Alex ready for the street celebrations, 1989.

closeness of the players. Perhaps it is the two matching stands, now unique in the UK. Maybe it is the front facade of the East Stand, or the view down Avenell Road from Aubert Park on match days. On the other hand, maybe it is the wonderful memories.

Best match ever: 3–0 v Anderlecht, April 1970. The first time I saw Arsenal win a trophy.

Best occasion: 4–0 v Everton, May 1998. Winning the championship on home soil.

Comeback of all time: drawing 4–4 with Spurs after being 0–4 down in the first half, October 1962.

Matches best forgotten: 2–5 v Spartak Moscow, September 1982; 2–6 v Manchester United, November 1990.

BRIAN BUSHBY

Heady days in a sober suit

I was born in Islington, a mile and a half from the stadium, and was first taken to see a reserve game by my father in the 1951–52 season. We went in the West Upper Stand and my abiding memory is of the seemingly endless climb up flights of stairs until we gazed down on the pitch from a dizzy height. It was a daunting prospect for a 10-year-old lad and I observed the same expressions of awe and excitement more than 20 years later when I took two young nephews along the same route.

After I had been coming to Highbury for a few years, I was amazed to learn that my father had walked into the ground and asked for a trial when he was a teenager. This had been back in 1922 – Arsenal had been admitted to the First Division only a few years previously (at the expense of Tottenham) and had yet to win any major trophy. Finding a gate open he walked in and interrupted a training session being conducted by the manager, Leslie Knighton. He explained that he played for Metrogas, the works team of the Metropolitan Gas Light and Coke Company, as a forward and would like to play for Arsenal. Mr Knighton was impressed by his initiative and advised him to write to Arsenal a few days before he was due to play so that a scout could be sent along to watch him.

My father never followed up this offer – I think he realised his own limitations as a player and he never tried to claim that he could have set Herbert Chapman a selection problem a few years later by worrying who to drop to accommodate him out of Hulme, Jack, Lambert, James or Bastin! But he appreciated how he was treated with kindness and respect by the club.

I was hooked from my first visit, when Arsenal scored seven against Brighton and Hove Albion (I relished their full title) with left winger James Robertson running riot before eventually being carried off after colliding with a goalpost. He moved to Brentford soon afterwards as part of the transfer deal that brought Tommy Lawton to Highbury. I waited until 1954 for my first league match, losing 1–0 to Portsmouth on a day when four of our players were on international duty for Wales.

Of course, we had just entered a spell of 17 years without a trophy, but there were consolations. The 1955 game against Blackpool which ended 4–1 in our favour when someone in the crowd blew a whistle and our left back, Dennis Evans, jubilantly slammed the ball past our own goalkeeper Sullivan, thinking it was the end of the game – so excited that he had overcome Stanley Matthews on the Blackpool side.

In 1958 we lost 5–4 to Manchester United in the last game they played in England before the Munich disaster which cost the lives of the Busby Babes. As we had fought back from three goals down, this remains one of the greatest games ever witnessed at Highbury.

A very evocative memory of my visits to the Stadium in the Fifties is the smell of the cigarette smoke at a time when about half the spectators were smoking, particularly at half-time. In the gloom, cigarette lighters would flicker like fireflies and a blue haze would rise to hover above the pitch, trapped in the glare of the floodlights. The one exception was the home fixture at Christmas, when the richer and more seasonal aroma of cigars was easily detected.

In 1968 and 1969 I was at Wembley to see us lose two successive League Cup Finals, first to Leeds by a single disputed goal and then to Swindon, an outstanding Third Division team who were promoted that year.

But 17 years of frustration were ended in 1970 on the evening of 28th April. Arsenal had reached the final of the European Fairs Cup against Anderlecht of

Belgium, who held a 3–1 lead from the first leg. I travelled straight from my office in my sober suit and tie to take up my position on the open terrace at the Clock End in the crowd that grew to 51,612 by kick-off.

The visitors came closest to scoring before Eddie Kelly gave us a 1–0 advantage at half time with a 20-yard shot. The tension was almost unbearable as Arsenal pounded the Anderlecht defence, then Bob McNab crossed from the left and John Radford rose above everyone to head the ball home. Almost straight from the restart Arsenal surged back at our shocked opponents and John Sammels fired in a third goal. The wait for the final whistle seemed endless but, when it came, the crowd erupted. Some fans were in tears, but I was capering around with the complete stranger who had been standing next to me.

There would be many celebrations over the next thirty years, not least our first Double, then only 12 months away. But somehow, nothing would quite live up to that evening. It was at Highbury and I had waited 17 years for success. It then paved the way for the team and fans to believe that even greater things would be achieved. The next day back at work was pretty good too. My suit was still sober, but it was the exception to the rule.

JOHN PARISH

A touch of fever

When I was married it was understood that if Arsenal were playing then I would attend, and all domestic arrangements would take that into account, including Christmas Day and holidays – even family weddings. It was not so easy for my brother-in-law, who suffered domestic turmoil every time he came with me to a match. Only with great difficulty could he attend home fixtures. But in those days we were all hard up, and my brother-in-law had the only car in which we travelled to away games.

ABOVE

Highbury Corner, scene of many passing celebrations.

76

In January 1962 Arsenal were drawn away to play Manchester United in the fourth round of the FA Cup, and I managed to obtain four tickets. My brother-in-law had managed to obtain permission, so we all looked forward to the trip up north.

Then one day my sister was reading the paper and noticed that someone had died of smallpox in Manchester.

All hell broke out in my brother-in-law's house,

"You are not going up there, where they're all dying!" She had a tendency to over-exaggerate.

"But we can't waste these tickets," he said. "In any event, I've been vaccinated."

"But I haven't," she exploded.

After much to-ing and fro-ing he managed to persuade her to be vaccinated along with their son. My wife and son and other family members were also visiting doctors for the dreaded jabs. We were not very popular.

The great day came with my sister lying ill in bed with a temperature of 104 degrees from the vaccination, and the four of us setting off for Manchester.

It was long before the M6 was built and I remember the weather was fine all the way to Congleton. We then noticed a distinct change in the climate, with flares alight on the side of the road. In Manchester it was cold and foggy but still clear enough for the match to be played. Some 60,000 packed the ground when thick clumps of fog poured in from the Stretford End. With half an hour to go and the team stripped ready to play, the game was called off.

We stopped at a pub on the journey home for refreshment.

My brother-in-law started to laugh. He could see the funny side of it all.

"God's punishment, that's what she'll say."

As we walked into his house, a voice from the sickbed upstairs shouted down: "God's punishment."

Oh, by the way, the Gunners lost 1–0 in the rearranged match. But we were not there.

BELOW
John Parish outside his "Highbury" home.

WHEN
SATURDAY,
SUNDAY OR MONDAY NIGHT
COMES...

ABOVE

Entrance to the West Stand.

LEFT

Highbury prepares.

OPPOSITE

Best meal of the day,

Match day!

LEFT

Hanging out the washing.

Make sure it's red.

ABOVE

*The box office brings
bad news.*

RIGHT

*All quiet in the tunnel,
for now.*

BELOW

*First fans arrive and check
out the street stalls around
Avenell Road.*

LEFT

*The Stewards' room, next
to the Clock End.*

ABOVE

*Has anyone seen my
jacket?*

RIGHT

Stewards check the aisles in the North Bank Upper, as they do before every game.

ABOVE

A chance for the stewards to get out of the rain for a while in the team dugout.

THE MAGIC BOX

Before match day comes around and the fans begin their journey to Highbury, the planning for televising the game begins. While the Arsenal squad prepares for the coming match at their training ground at Shenley, in Hertfordshire, the Sky TV machine swings into action. Arriving at the ground 36 hours before kick-off they begin to lay the eight miles of cable required by the cameras around the pitch's perimeter. In total 22 cameras are placed in key locations, and it takes a full day to complete the outside broadcast installation.

A team of over a hundred personnel sets up the unit, and by match day the Clock End car park is crammed with eight TV trucks, from articulated lorry to transit van. Tucked away from public gaze, the Sky team prepares for their live link-up later that day. The production area is self-sufficient, with back-up

RIGHT
*The Steady-Cam sweeps
along the touchline.*

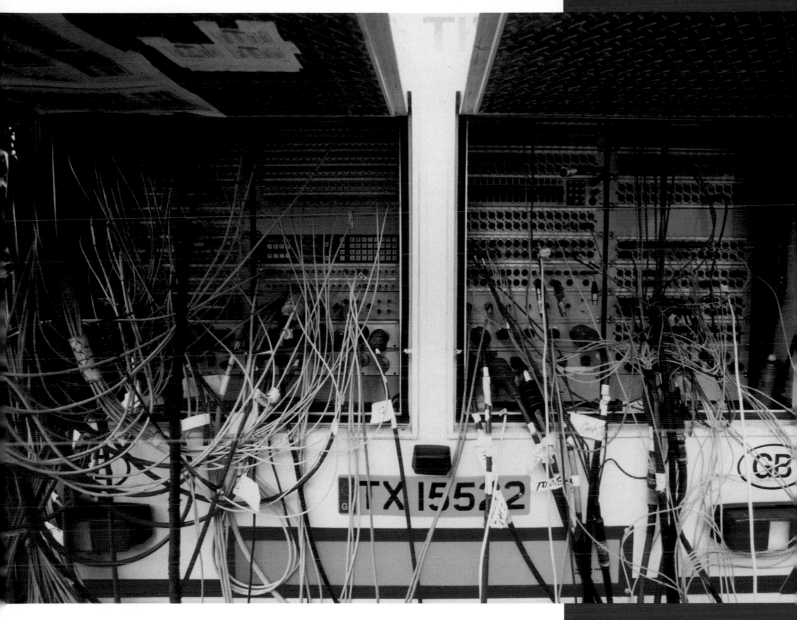

generators in the event of a power failure. Remember the blackout at Wimbledon in 1997?

With an hour to go before kick-off, the two teams ready themselves in the changing rooms and the ground begins to fill with supporters. Meanwhile pre-match interviews with football pundits are conducted at pitch side, and outside the ground the milling supporters are quizzed for their match views.

With kick-off ever closer, the camera team is ready, and the Steady-Cam

ABOVE

Microphones are set up around the pitch perimeter to capture the Highbury roar.

operator is positioned at pitch level to follow the teams out. This camera, mounted on a body harness and fitted with a gyroscope that allows it to stay level at all time, produces sweeping movement images and is able to follow an exciting breakaway or counter-attack from the fan's eye view. During the game the Mini-Cam located behind each goalmouth will record the goals from yet another viewpoint – even though it is only the size of a mug of tea.

The match director controls both the selection of camera angles and the commentators' input throughout the ninety minutes. And as the game is played out in front of the Highbury faithful, millions more will join them from around the globe through pictures beamed back to the viewer's dish via a satellite orbiting 23,500 miles above the earth.

The Premiership link-up with Sky Broadcasting in the early Nineties completely transformed football on the box, and the way we see the game has changed even further with the advent of digital television.

Imagine how we will be watching Arsenal once the new twenty-first century has got into its stride.

BELOW
It can be a long wait for the Sky TV crew.

RIGHT
*Sky's Richard Keys gets
Frank McLintock's views
before the game.*

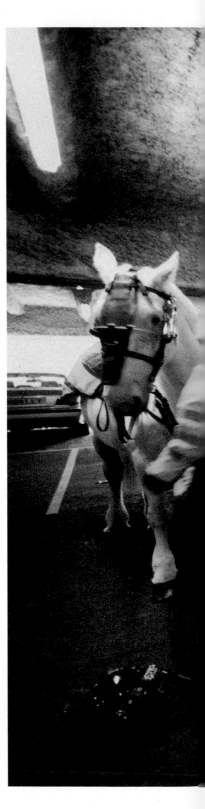

ABOVE

Police horses unloaded in Drayton Park.

RIGHT

The St John Ambulance, ready for any emergency.

FAR RIGHT

Mounted police prepare beneath the Clock End.

LEFT

The North Bank bar as we never have seen it – empty.

FAR LEFT

Time to open the doors?

BELOW

West Stand Lower, ready.

UPPER TIER

DOUBLE TOP

George Graham heading for goal with John Radford close at hand. Arsenal v Rouen, Fairs Cup, 1970.

KEN BANHAM

Making merry with The Mob

Here are some of the great matches I have seen and been involved with. They have also had a great bearing on Arsenal's history and standing in world football.

I have been an active supporter since 1953, my father since 1926, my sons 1978 and 1986. You can see most of us got involved in years that the club won something.

The first big match for me as a young man came after the two bad defeats in the old League Cup: the first against Leeds, when Jim Furnell was impeded by Jack Charlton, then most of our players going down with flu the week of the Swindon final. Not to mention the Wembley pitch – it was so muddy due to a horse show the week before, when extra time came the heavy bog of the pitch sapped our players. What we did not know at that terrible time of sadness in defeat was that we were building a great team for the future.

So the match against Anderlecht became so important for us supporters. I was in Highbury Grange with a lot of Arsenal supporters listening to the first leg of the semi-final on a car radio. We could not believe that we were three down until Ray Kennedy came on as sub and scored that late goal – we all felt then that the second leg would be ours. We just needed two goals at home – our defence was just showing signs of greatness.

So to the big day – we all met in the Gunners pub. We knew the crowd would be big, so we went into the North Bank early. We did not stop singing, the crowd were fantastic. Well of course we won 3–0 – we all got on the pitch and Charlie George was just about to swap shirts with an Anderlecht player when my mate John Hoy grabbed it. He went to Holloway School with Charlie – well, we did the conga on the pitch and the whole of Highbury was going mad. We then went to the Robinson Crusoe pub, where we danced on the tables and sang until closing time. Then at least thirty came to my house, in Highbury New Park, to watch the match on TV with my dad – Mr Arsenal. All the lads around the Highbury area called him that as he was always telling them about the club and how great they were, and most importantly about the Arsenal way and tradition.

We did not know then, but the seeds had been planted. The next season was just about the greatest of all time.

My pals and I went up to Hillsborough for the semi-final [against Stoke City] about thirty-handed, as we always were. Well, we could not believe it at half time – we were two down. In the second half Peter Storey scored with a lovely drive but it seemed we were going out when from a corner in the last minute Frank McLintock headed goalwards and John Mahoney hand-balled it – Penalty! But wait a minute, Peter Storey was going to have to take it against Gordon Banks – probably the world's best goalie at the time. A lot of my pals could not look. I had to. Well… the rest is history, we went crazy.

And so to the Leeds league match, three games to go in the season. This was an evening game. My dad Ken Banham senior and my cousin John Peck and the same mob set off – but our train had a fire in one carriage and we had to stop, at Crewe I believe. This of course delayed us.

Well, when you get to Leeds you have to pass the ground and go into the centre and then come back out again. All we could see was thousands of people, and someone said "We will never get in if we go into Leeds," so my pal John Hoy pulled the emergency cord. Everyone got off, and I remember running across a field and my dad and me just stopped to look behind and all you could see was the train driver, just standing there with all the doors open and the sunset behind. I don't think I will ever forget that. Well, we lost that one – I believe to an offside goal by our old enemy Jack Charlton.

On to our last league game, to draw nil–nil or win, at Tottenham of all places. We knew there would be a massive crowd. So we all took the day off and got to the Park Lane entrance at about 10.30am. We had someone to go and get chips and drinks, the gates opened about 6pm.

I was one of the first in and the Park Lane End became the North Bank. We did not stop singing, we knew this was ours. With about nine with ten minutes to go, for just a minute the tension was at an all-time high. The Park Lane End stopped singing, and beginning at the Paxton Road End, then around the ground, the sound of "When the Reds go marching in" could be heard – the ground was full of Arsenal supporters! Only about six thousand season ticket holders for Tottenham, there weren't so many in those days.

Then big Ray Kennedy headed us in front and of course we danced on the Tottenham pitch of all places. The Tottenham police were pretty rough, they threw me straight on to the concrete terrace from the pitch, but it was worth it. We marched up Tottenham High Road to Manor House, where we went in and danced on the tables – we were The Champions and we did it at Tottenham.

So on to Wembley – what a hot day, we just kept singing "We are the Champions" and "Good old Arsenal". We should have won in normal time, we missed so many chances. Into extra time, and Liverpool take the lead – but somehow you know we will not lose. Then the equaliser – Eddie Kelly hits it in, George Graham claims it. Then to King Charlie's great goal – what a winner! From an Islington lad, the same as all of us.

In the queue for the tube at Wembley I was totally shattered and these scouse said to me "We cannot understand you. You have just won the Double and you are not singing." I said in a croaky voice "I have not stopped singing since Monday night from our win at Tottenham." As we got off the tube at Arsenal we kissed the stairs of the stadium.

Next to the Gunners pub, sank a few pints and then the songs began, again – at closing time the whole of Blackstock Road did the conga – me on my pal Dave Pooley's shoulders – even the police were dancing. Finally to the Town Hall for the parade. Another great day, all the families came out – mums, wives, babies – all done up, drinking all day. Then I became a father and even more success followed.

Now Arsène Wenger has come – great football, a great double in '98 – almost did it again in '99. Let's hope the future has as much excitement as the past years have. It most certainly has been my family's life – great times, great moments and a great club.

The Mob:

Ken Banham Snr	Ken Banham Jnr	John Peck
John Hoy	Gordon Neale	Lenny Togwell
Tony Baker	Gary Davis	Dennis Phillip
Ian Graham	Malcolm Froy	Micky Putney
Eddie Symes	Colin T	George Flack
Colin Walgrove	Dave and Vicky Pooley	Scatty Don

Billy Truefitt	Bobby Matton	Charlie Douglas
Kevin Douglas	John Hayes	Bootsey
Frank Warren	Ray Morrish	Peter Kennedy
Brian and Terry Jacobs	Colin Gregory	Ian Quelch
Silly John	Suzie King	Jacky
Johnnie Javarni	Algie Sculley	Chrissy King
Bob Jones		

TOM KINSELLA

Red letter day

This letter was written on 5th May 1971 by Tom Kinsella to his pen friend in Ireland, Bernard Tymlin.

Yes Old Son,

You can believe it. We are The Greatest. What a week. I haven't gotten over it yet.

I have aged years with tension. I only wish I had the gift of being able to put on paper my feelings and I am sure the feelings of every Arsenal fan. But I am going to have a go.

Spurs v Arsenal

I knocked off work at 3.15 and arrived at the ground at about 4.15. There were about 10,000 people there that early. We got into the ground at 5.30, ate our sandwiches and waited.

The team came out to look over the pitch and suddenly all Tottenham ground seemed covered in red and white. It was fantastic!

The gates were closed an hour before kick-off. And so to the kick-off. We attacked from the word go and kept it up all night. Mullery did everything in his power to upset Charlie George. It took Frank McLintock to put him in his place. Frank McLintock – what can one say about the man? He made Chivers look foolish, as he has made every centre forward look all through the season. As the game wore on the strain on the lads must have been terrific.

9 Wooding Grove
Harlow
Essex
17/5/71

Yes Old Son

You can believe it "We are the greatest" What a week. I havent gotten over it yet. I have aged years with tension. ...

Spurs v Arsenal

I knocked off work 3.15 & arrived at ... ground at about 4.15 There was about 10,000 there that early. ... into the ground at 5... our sandwiches & waite... The team came out ... over the pitch & ... all Tottenham ground to be covered in ... It was fantastic. The gates were closed ... before kick off. ... to the kick off. We attacked from ... go & kept it up ...

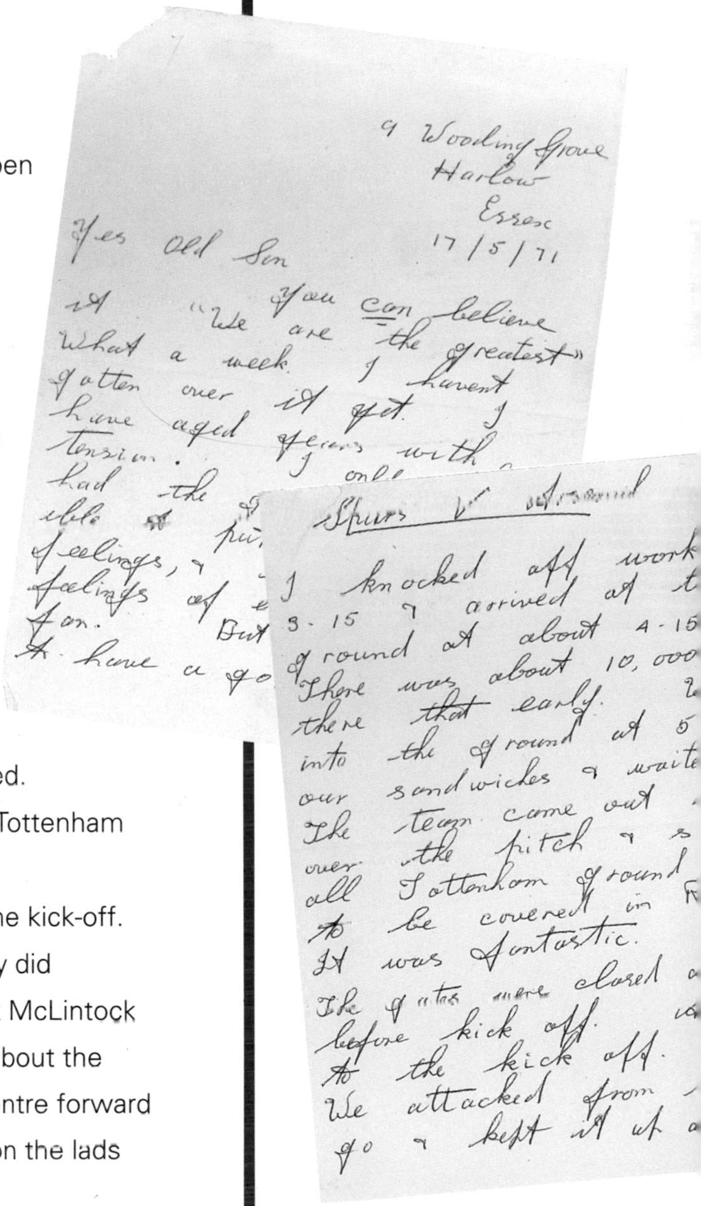

Can you imagine it? They dare not let Spurs score. Yet they must try to score themselves to win the League on points and not goal average. Spurs mounted attack after attack but our defence and Bob the great kept them out. By this time I was really sweating and tense. Then came the great moment. A partial clearance by Jennings, a lob back into the area and there was our Golden Boy Ray. "Bang". We had scored!

Can you imagine me, a grandfather, jumping, shouting, singing like a teenager. You know something I felt proud to be alive and supporting the finest team in England. Then the final whistle. We had won the Championship. "We are the Champions."

The crowd went mad. One of my mates was out on his feet, tears streaming down his face. He threw his arms around me and we both had a good cry. After all the years of waiting I had at last seen my team pull off a fantastic feat. To beat Spurs at home and take the Championship to boot is something I shall never forget. I felt honoured to be there on such a great occasion. Having reached our cars after fighting our way through delirious fans we went to a pub in Epping. I didn't get home until 4.15. Half drunk and hoarse. But happy!

WEMBLEY 8TH MAY 1971

Never forget that date.

We left Harlow by car at 9.30 and drove to South London to where the rest of the gang lived. When we arrived at John's flat he had a red and white flag and the Union Jack draped over the balcony. Arsenal pictures in every window. The Arsenal song blaring all over Balham. It was great.

After a cup of tea we marched (all 15 of us) to the tube station, flags flying, scarves waving and singing our heads off. When we got into the tube there was a crowd of Liverpudlians in it. So we all started to sing our own team songs and by heavens son we out-sang them. They were a great crowd of lads.

When we got to Wembley the crowd was enormous. Once again we got the flags out and marched up Olympic Way.

At last we were inside Wembley and the scene was fantastic. Red and white flags and scarves against gold and blue. Liverpool voices against Arsenal and our two Irish voices. Sun shining and everyone singing and sweating but tense, waiting for the big moment. At last it came. The noise was deafening. The whistle and we were off. The papers gave you a fair account of the play. If we'd gone in at half time 3–0 up we would not have been flattered. We played the best football, made the best chances but Ray missed a few sitters. For the first 20 minutes George Graham looked as if he was out for an afternoon stroll. Then he was ripping the Liverpool defence to shreds. Hitting the bar, having shots cleared off the line. We went on singing and sweating.

Radford was playing like a Trojan but he was getting no change out of Smith. Charlie George cracked in shots that had to pay off in the end. Still we kept singing and by now we were singing Liverpool out of it. Then the 90-minute whistle. Visions of Swindon looming up, but we kept singing and by this time I had my shirt off. I am getting too old for this kind of tension.

The start of extra time. Bertie and Don had been around our lads urging them to greater efforts. Suddenly out of nothing Heighway scored. A lot of people blamed Wilson for being out of position. I didn't see it that way. Heighway had made many a lone run like this before and always crossed to the middle. Wilson moved out to cut off the cross and Heighway saw the small gap and fired. A good goal.

And what a blessing it was to us. Frank ran among his players shouting, urging them on and by heavens it paid off.

A lob by Radford, a Kelly challenge and the ball was in the net. After that it was all Arsenal. Radford found Smith's weak spot and played on it. Frank made Toshack look like an amateur. A couple of minutes to go plus injury time, still 1–1. We went on singing and sweating and by now the Liverpool song birds were very quiet. We had won the song contest, now let us get on with winning the football contest. We were masters in midfield and at the back, now let's get our forwards going. And go they did. A cross from the wing. Charlie George pulls it down with his left foot, hit it with his right and "Wham". There was no stopping us now. I did not see what happened in the next two minutes. I was on my knees trying to lift George up. He had fainted.

Then it was all over. We had done the Double. I just can't explain my feelings. I was sore, hoarse, thirsty and whacked but by heavens I felt 20 years younger. To see my team carrying the FA Cup around Wembley, to see Bob Wilson conducting the North Bank choir and all the lads dancing and singing, carrying King Francis on their shoulders was a sight that will live in my memory for a long time.

We went back to John's place for a party which kept going to 4.30. We staggered back to Harlow in time for breakfast.

Well old son, I am getting cramp so I will have to close.

Write soon.

Tom

BERNARD CHAPLIN

Toast to an absent friend

This is the story of two soccer supporters who became friends through their love of following the Arsenal together for nearly forty years.

Arthur Booth and I started out on the terraces and eventually, after a year or two on the waiting list, obtained season tickets together in the East Stand Lower. Our debut sitting down was a home loss against Ipswich.

Many memories were shared over the years, with both highs and lows.

I remember walking home despondently after the loss against Swindon in the League Cup final of '69, thinking that the club would never win anything after the wilderness years. Arsenal had been hot favourites for the game but happened to meet their opponents on the worst Wembley pitch ever, a goalkeeper who played the game of his life and a team that were exhausted through a bout of 'flu that had hit the club in the previous week or so.

Next we experienced two high points. The Fairs Cup win followed by the Double. That night at White Hart Lane will never be forgotten. We left work early, in good time we thought, but the streets around the ground were absolutely crowded. However, we managed to get within a few feet of the entrance when we had to give up trying to get in, believing that we would be crushed. Presence of the police had no effect in controlling the crowd. The next ninety minutes were spent wandering outside the ground listening to transistor radios. A few minutes from the end the gates opened for early leavers. We rushed in and were just in time to see the winning goal. After the match we invaded the pitch for the first and only time. There were tears all round, even from grown men. And at White Hart Lane!

Other highs and lows included being scared to death when Glasgow Rangers visited in 1967 and ran riot. Being soaked to the skin at Portsmouth for a Cup tie in 1970. Driving back from Wolverhampton in a snowstorm. Visiting Gillingham, after work, to watch a League Cup match and hardly seeing any action because of fog. Arsenal winning 5–0 at the Lane just before Christmas.

We reached our last high point, the win in the Cup-Winners Cup against Parma. Shortly after this Arthur was diagnosed as having cancer. He did not survive to see the defence of the Cup or the great days that have returned with Arsène Wenger.

LEFT
Arthur Booth sitting in his East Stand Lower seat.

ABOVE
Bernard Chaplin in front of the West Stand.

W. TRUEFITT

Heavy hearts

It was back in 1973, in the days when travelling fans could count on buying a ground ticket on the day of the match.

The 1971 Double-winning side was almost still intact. The venue we were heading for was Maine Road, and it was a cold, overcast November morning. There were four of us travelling in a Ford Consul along the M1 from London. As we joined the M6, we were divided into three lanes – the central lane was for overtaking by either side.

As we overtook a hay lorry, my companions in our car yelled, "Look at this maniac!" In the central lane heading towards us was a Rover, with its lights full on, travelling at an incredible speed. I looked behind through the back window and saw a two-seater sports car behind us, with red and white scarves trailing from their windows, smash head on with the Rover.

They had no chance to avoid the fatal accident.

We pulled over and my friend and I from the rear seat ran back to see what we could do to help. The sports car was a write off – the passenger was able to speak and asked us to get him out of the car. We laid him on the ground and he asked if his friend was OK. We said he was being taken care of, but in reality he had died instantly.

The ambulance arrived shortly after, and when he had been put inside he asked me if, as he wasn't able to make the match, I would reach into his jeans pocket and accept two tickets he had for the game with thanks for the help we had given him.

We reached the ground with heavy hearts and in a very sorry state. We sat in the seats, watching the match in the rain, the mud-sodden pitch of Man City sapping the strength of the players.

But as I sat watching Eddie Kelly and Brian Hornsby score the goals to give Arsenal a 2–1 victory, my thoughts were with the two young supporters who suffered this tragedy to follow and watch their idols.

I still think of them to this day.

If the surviving passenger reads this, I would like to hear how he is getting on.

N. PARTRIDGE KING

Spying for the Communists

At last, Arsenal had qualified to play in Europe [the 1978/79 Uefa Cup] and now that I was in full time work I could afford to see them play away. In the first round we were drawn against Lokomotiv Leipzig (then behind the Iron Curtain in East Germany) and I could hardly wait to go. I persuaded my father, who incidentally saw us win the FA Cup in 1936 and who was currently working in central London, to book for me through David Dryer – there was no Travel Club yet in existence.

The first surreal thing to happen was at work. As I was then, and alarmingly still am, in the Civil Service, my boss – a fifty-something-year-old and a rather formidable battle-axe – was required to warn me not to get involved with any East German prostitutes, as evidence of this could be used as a lever to force me to spy for the Communists.

The coaches – I believe there were two – left from Drayton Park station and the journey was fairly uneventful for a while. Then we hit Belgium, a comparatively small country you would think, which seemed to take hours and hours to get through – I swear we went through Brussels about six hours after having left it. As a result of this we were seriously concerned that we might be late for the game.

The excitement of Leipzig in 1978.

The next excitement was not surprisingly on the East German border – it comes as quite a shock when you first see machine guns pointing at you. However, we crossed without a hitch but made up for that an hour later. Driving on the autobahn at a sensible speed, suddenly three motor cycles overtook us in a blaze of flashing blue lights. We pulled over and were told that we were going no further until a spot fine for speeding was paid. Our driver was thankfully a realist, if not a great navigator, and paid up with little or no argument.

We eventually arrived at the Zentral station in Lepzig less than half an hour before kick-off. The huge stadium was totally without any cover and the rain was torrential. If you were at Huddersfield or Barnsley a few years ago, you'll get the idea. More important, the team turned on a great performance including Frank Stapleton's Irish hat-trick – two in their net and one in ours. During the game, quite a number of locals mixed in with the small band of Gunners. Many were supporters of Lokomotiv's local rivals, Leipzig Chemicals, and some were local members of the Leipzig anti-Communist league. And there was one East German army officer who was significantly under the influence of alcohol.

I don't quite know how, but by getting a few Arsenal scarves together we persuaded him to swap his army hat. Encouraged by this success, we gathered together a really big number of scarves and tried to persuade the same officer to swap his handgun. We very nearly succeeded, but it's probably just as well we didn't.

After the game we were taken to our rather posh hotel in the centre of the city. The normal clientele, very stuffy and dour-looking Eastern bloc businessmen in the main, seemed shocked and alarmed to see us. Forty or fifty soaked, unwashed in thirty-six hours, hungry but elated Arsenal supporters liberally decked out in red and white in their lobby. Having cleaned up and eaten a tasty (though unidentified) meal, we were discussing what to do next when to our delight Terry Neill arrived at the hotel specifically to say thank you for the support. I still have a picture of myself with my arm around the manager's neck.

So how do you follow that? Well, what you do is wander about the deserted city centre singing football songs and by pure luck find yourselves outside the hotel where the players and officials are celebrating, get yourselves invited in and spend an hour and a half swapping stories and jokes with your heroes. Ecstasy!

How we ever found our way back to our hotel I have no idea, but obviously we did. The following morning we had a couple of hours to spend in Leipzig before facing the journey home. The one significant event to happen on the way home was (again not surprisingly) on the East German border. The machine guns were still pointing at us, there were mirrors on the road so that the guards could see that no one was clinging to the underside of the coach… and there was some maniacal supporter, wearing the army hat, goose-stepping, straight-arm saluting, up and down the aisle. I was convinced that we were all going to be taken out and shot there and then. However, the guards seemed to shrug their shoulders, mutter something like "verdammte Englische Schweine" and waved us through in record time.

ALLEN LUCAS

She wore a yellow ribbon

Everyone remembers the game as The Five-Minute Final as United pulled back a two-goal deficit only to be beaten by Alan Sunderland's spectacular last-gasp winner down at our end. Yes!

But the truth was that for eighty minutes we had totally bossed the game with Liam Brady spraying passes or dropping his shoulder and dribbling almost at will. The fashion in the picture is just how it was. Dig the flares and curly hair – like punk never happened. Unusually, I'm only wearing one scarf – generally I had a couple of silk ones tied round my wrists. The badges under my belt are Brady, Rix and Stapleton.

What a great young team we had then – and so did the Arsenal. That Final was a moment to relish, when you look back you always remember the sun shining on yellow ribbon days in May. It really did back then, I promise.

ABOVE

"Off to Wembley!" The 1979 FA Cup Final. On the left Steve Mann, centre Roy Poole and right "Spam".

LEFT

Allen, on the right, on the way to Wembley, 1979.

ABOVE

"Operation Gunner" – Steve Mann on the right and Roy "Scarfie" Poole on the left. On board the cross-channel ferry moving 25,000 Gunners to Belgium.

MICK GRAY

One night in a Commer van

I had been married one year, although only twenty-two and living in a maisonette in Enfield. It was 1980. The second leg of the Cup-Winners Cup semi-final brings back vivid memories, as does the subsequent trip to the final. My wife and I had a friend over that night and of course I had the stereo on listening to the Juventus game.

Then Vaessen scores, 1–0 to the Arsenal. Yes! I am off to Belgium, "da, da, da, da" as I went dancing round the room. My wife's friend must have thought I was loopy. The trip couldn't come round quick enough for me and the party of guys who were all going along. We hired an old Commer van, fourteen-seater – with thirteen going it would be tight, especially as big Chrissy Parker took up two seats on his own. We set off two clear days before the match, making Dover with no trouble.

Geoff and Graham were doing the driving as they were years older than the rest of us and had more driving experience and read maps well – don't you believe it! As soon as we got across the Channel it was "which way do we go now?" Follow that car or that one? Travelled for a while passing this and that and I'm sure to this day we were going round in circles. Anyway we came across a sports ground, I am sure we were still in France at the time. We pulled up, got the football out and started to have a kickaround which lasted the afternoon. Evening came and we settled down for the night in the sports complex. In the early hours the police arrived, rounded us up and moved us on. So once again we were on the road, this time in the dark. It was mind-blowing where we would end up, with everyone arguing about which way to go.

Then dawn broke, and believe it or not we were in Belgium, not only Belgium but Brussels. We had arrived. We parked up straight at the first fountain and brushed our teeth in it. Some locals passed by, and must have thought what the…?

ABOVE AND LEFT
*Warming up before the
game in Brussels, 1980.*

The atmosphere on the day was fantastic. The bars were packed solid, singing, chanting, what a bunch of nutters – happy to be there having a great time. I remember going out to the toilet, walking into this big room with a hole in the floor. Yes, that was it. I looked round and there's a woman on a pay phone in the corner... weird – beaten only by the one at Preston North End in '99, a flickering-light cesspit.

We entered the ground – well, what an eye-opener. The terracing was crumbling and falling apart, not the best of venues, I must say. The game was not bad, Arsenal had the chances to win in 90 minutes but it was not to be... penalties and defeat. Arsenal were too dejected to come over to us at the end of the game. It would have been nice, but you can't blame them.

Then suddenly to my right the fence between the standing and seating sections started to move and it was down. The boys were going in. It didn't last long, a bit of argy-bargy, just a couple of hot-heads. Disappointed, we made the decision to go straight home, collected a couple of Spanish flags pulled from a passing car – must have got caught up with someone's arms.

Then the port, ferry, home and the morning papers, to read what might have been.

STEVE CASSIDY

The unofficial Highbury tour

Arsenal Football Club, the Marble Halls, the North Bank, Junior Gunners, the priceless season ticket and Perry Groves!

Over my whole life to date the above have contributed to so many memories. My association with the Arsenal started when I was nine years old – my father took me to the game against Ipswich in 1980. Perched behind the goal, I took to

the noise straightaway. The noise, atmosphere and the spontaneous crowd reactions of the 42,000 meant I couldn't wait to go again – a day that will stay with me for a long while.

I remember my father took my two brothers and me on a tour of Arsenal Stadium at around the same time. Little did I know then that it was to play a significant part in my life for the next 14 years. We sat in the dugout with the Arsenal Stadium cat Gunner. That was an official tour of Highbury, but there would be an unofficial tour in 1986. My brother and I were Junior Gunners and regular Highbury-goers. I was picked to play in a Junior Gunners team against the Junior Hammers, so my brother and myself trained down on the Cambridge to Finsbury Park line. Sadly we lost 5–1, but afterwards went through an open entrance in the Clock End and suddenly there we were, standing in the Clock End goalmouth in the pitch dark – Unbelievable!

To follow our unofficial tour, on the way back to Finsbury Park the main entrance was open and we decided to go in. I had my camera so I took a couple of quick photos of Stuart and two other Junior Gunners outside the Trophy Room. We all ran out chanting "Arsenal, Arsenal". It did surprise me that here were 13- and 14-year-olds walking around Arsenal Stadium with no-one even noticing us.

One of my most satisfying days at Arsenal was an FA Cup fifth-round tie against Manchester United, 20th February 1988. A massive 54,161 crowd and it was not all-ticket. From the moment we all stepped off the train at Finsbury Park, the atmosphere was really buzzing. The tie came hot on the heels of an encounter in the league a month before, also at home. Fortunately for them they had won 2–1, with the referee disallowing two good Arsenal goals. The Gunners had a score to settle and achieved it in such a thrilling way it will never be forgotten.

The North Bank was full – we had got there early to secure our usual spot, below halfway, left hand side of the goal. After the first half we were strolling 2–0 up and rejoicing, swaying, singing and thoroughly enjoying beating United. Drama was to follow. Brian McClair pulled a goal back right in front of us just after the restart. The game was now wide open and Michael Thomas had an effort saved (he was to make amends, of course, next season). The noise now was deafening, with quick chances for both sides.

Then with only a few minutes to go United were awarded a penalty. No! It can't be! But it was. McClair again, to take the game to a replay. John Lukic dived the wrong way, but McClair planted the ball firmly into the North Bank. The place went delirious. It was bedlam from then on and after the game, all the way back to Cambridge.

Now my ambition is to take my two boys, Nicholas and Lewis, to Arsenal in the future.

JON LEE

Work very hard at school

I wrote to Arsenal in 1981 to see if I could play for them. At that time I was nine and had no idea how old you had to be. Arsenal sent this reply and signed team sheets. I was convinced they were going to come and watch me play for my team. I became an Arsenal fan in 1978, aged six. I remember feeling so sad and low when we lost to Ipswich one–nil in the FA Cup that year. The rest is history, I've been a fan ever since.

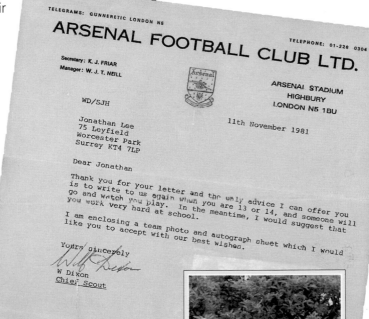

TOM CHAPMAN

From Somerset... with hope

Back in the mid-Eighties, during my most intense period of being a travelling away-Gunner, I had come up the M4 from my Somerset backwater in the hope of witnessing a feast of goals against one of the weaker sides in the old First Division (I think it was either Birmingham City or Stoke). "Guaranteed Goals! Guaranteed Entertainment!" I used to kid myself.

Once again, we were treated to something so diabolical you simply had to be there to believe it. In fact, so inspired was the spectacle being dished out to the paltry 18,000 or so crowd, that up on the North Bank we were forced to look for alternative ways to entertain ourselves. The Gooners scattered across the patchy terraces had to content themselves by taking it in turns tossing their scarves and berets up into the rafters of the roof. Those who succeeded in doing so got as big a cheer as the ref's final whistle. The game finished 0–0 and it rained all the way back to Victoria Bus Station.

Over and over I used to ask myself on those eternal journeys home why I did it. But I was sure that one day things would be different.

<u>ABOVE</u>
Tom endures another Eighties classic.

YENG

Anfield take-away

Arsenal versus Liverpool, the last match of the season, 1989. We were all at my mum and dad's shop, the Arsenal Fish Bar, all watching the match on TV.

When Michael Thomas scored, the whole place erupted. I was sitting with my sister and my dad. We all jumped up and hugged each other. None of us could believe it. When the final whistle went, everyone went berserk and ran out on to the streets to celebrate.

My family were the first ones on the street but within minutes the entire road was packed. Everyone was hugging each other, shaking hands and embracing, people who they didn't even know. We were all shouting and screaming along with the rest of the thousands of supporters.

People were driving up and down, hanging outside their windows, waving flags and scarves, just celebrating big time. It was just one huge party, an incredible scene. The celebrations went on for hours. We all lost our voices, we weren't tired at all, just on a high all night.

It was all worth it because for a lot of us it was one of the best days of our lives, a day we'll never ever forget.

LEFT

Celebrating outside the Arsenal Fish Bar, 1989.

90 MINUTES TO GO

ABOVE

Bergkamp's kit awaits him.

RIGHT

Vic Akers, Arsenal Kit Manager and Arsenal Ladies Manager, in the Home changing rooms just before the team arrives. All the first team kit is laid out on the right side and the substitutes on the left. Through the far door are the baths and boot room.

ABOVE AND LEFT

The stars of the boot room.

FAR LEFT

1. *Seaman*

2. *Dixon*

3. *Winterburn*

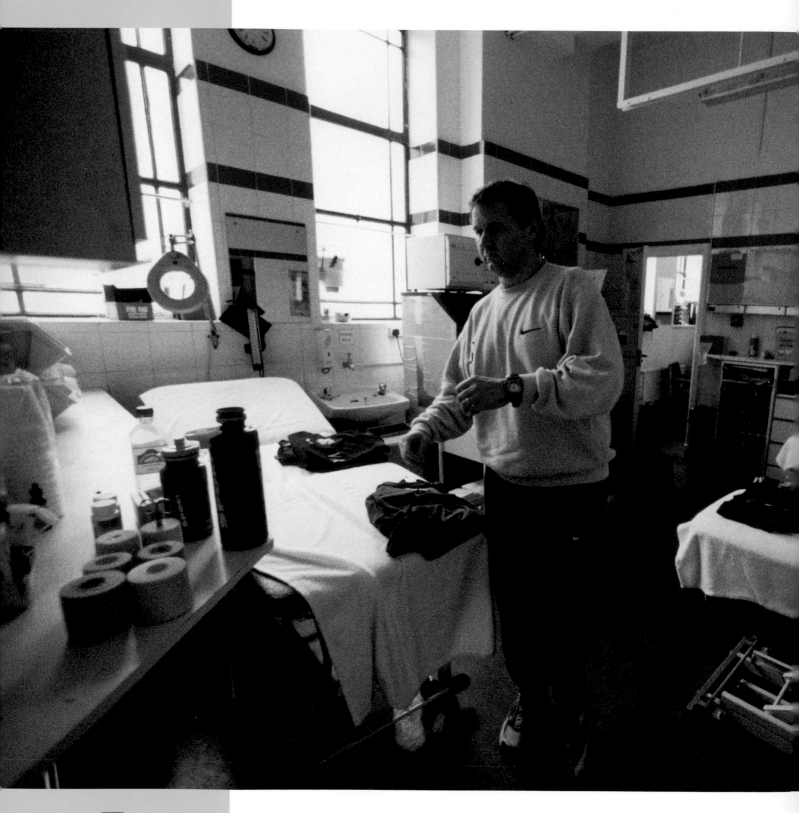

ABOVE
The baths waiting to be filled.

FAR LEFT
Gary Lewin – Physio for Arsenal and England – prepares.

LEFT
A well-stocked boot room.

125

SPEND, SPEND, SPEND

The World of Sport store – now approaching its tenth birthday – and the Gunners shop give every supporter the chance to buy Arsenal-related merchandise. To that end World of Sport alone employs 26 staff on match days – and one of them is John Paris. "Our best seller is the replica shirts, along with plenty of videos and, of course, books. The Nike polo shirts are a popular non-football item, but we try to avoid selling odd merchandise. I heard at Old Trafford they even sell Man Utd tomato sauce."

Two thousand people can visit the shop before a game. John explains: "You get to see all different classes of people here, the football fan goes from the millionaire to the person that sleeps on the street. Mums and dads buy more goods than the kids, but it's the kids who influence them. These days young girls are into football just as much as boys – and they can put some real pressure on their parents.

ABOVE

*Dennis Bergkamp has
another pressing
engagement.*

RIGHT

Two new kids on the park.

"We do get some adults who are kids, too. They come in and buy key rings, yo-yos, pencils — they're Arsenal mad. Once you're in love with the club that's it. It sticks."

John has been at the shop for six years and was overwhelmed with pride when the '98 Double was clinched. "It was the atmosphere in the shop amongst the staff. You just felt part of the club, as important as the players."

ABOVE
A young Gooner treats himself.

127

RIGHT

The gates are open and the ground slowly starts to fill.

ABOVE

Fans filter in to the Gillespie Road and Highbury Hill entrances.

RIGHT AND BELOW

We're in the North Bank!

RIGHT

The walk into the light, East Stand Lower.

ABOVE

How many times have I been here?

ABOVE AND LEFT

West Stand Upper – early arrivals.

ABOVE

Radio prepares in the upper East Stand.

RIGHT

West Stand media gantry ready for the evening game.

ABOVE AND RIGHT

Young Gooners enjoy a kickabout before the game on the Arsenal Soccer School training pitch, situated below the Clock End Stand.

Last chance to enjoy the hospitality of the North Bank before kick-off.

LEFT
Freddie Ljungberg meets some Junior Gunners.

LEFT
Arsenal TV edit suite behind the executive boxes in the Clock End – ready to replay the game's most exciting moments, action replays and goals.

ABOVE
Arsène Wenger announces Arsenal's line-up live on Jumbotron screen twenty minutes before kick-off.

JUNIOR GUNNERS
PEPSI
JUNIOR GUNNERS
JUNIOR GUNNERS
Gunners
SUKER
9

THE
GLORIOUS
NINETIES

LEFT

Another goal, another victory.

LUCA FRAZZI

A taste of Italy

Why do I support Arsenal, living in a small town in northern Italy called Fidenza? Because twenty years ago – it was August 1979 – my elder brother spent a holiday in London and returned with a gift of a red and white Arsenal scarf. Some months later, now fourteen years old, I watched on Italian television the Cup-Winners Cup semi-final between Arsenal and Juve. I saw Chippy Brady and Highbury. It was love at first sight.

Since then I have supported Arsenal in every way I can. I read English magazines and fanzines, I collect match programmes. I have a subscription to the official magazine and even listen to Sportsworld on the BBC World Service.

It's not easy to love a team like Arsenal and live so far from Highbury. On my first visit to London in '88 Arsenal played away, so I had to wait till '91. I then crowned my dream. I know that many people luckier than me in England can remember historic moments, the '71 double, the '79 Cup Final, Anfield '89, the Double in '98. Not me. I've seen only one match at Highbury. It was 26th October 1991. Arsenal v Notts County, 2–0, scored by Alan Smith and Ian Wright. I know it's not the most important game in Arsenal history, but it's important for me. I'll never forget the Highbury atmosphere, that incredible feeling.

Twenty years on and my life has changed, but I still have a photograph of Charlie George in my sitting room, and I love Arsenal like that far day in 1979, when my brother gave me that red and white scarf…

PAUL JOHNSON

Red and white wedding

I have been a devoted Arsenal supporter since the age of five. Such was my joy when we won the League in May 1991 that I proposed to my girlfriend, Alison.

We married in May 1992, after the football season. The colour scheme for the entire day was red and white – including the bride's dress. Even our dog, Guinness, attended and wore a large red collar and bow.

Our bridesmaid flew in from Texas the day before and had also managed to obtain an Arsenal-red dress.

AMANDA WALL

Party, party, party

I was born in 1971 and was only allowed to wear red and white or yellow and blue.

The 1997–1998 season, what a season… To win the league with that Tony Adams goal – just thinking about it makes me get goosebumps. The atmosphere was electric at Highbury and as number three went in it was party time. I remember the final whistle, the screaming, partying, Tony lifting the cup and then all the Arsenal fans pouring on to Avenell Road.

Tony was hanging out of the dressing-room window, singing with all the fans and introducing us to all the players and making them come to the window. He did lift Marcy up so we could see him. And I do remember singing, "Who the **** are Man United…" Then we went partying in town and into Football, Football to watch the goals again and we sang and sang – all around town you could hear Arsenal fans singing.

Then to top it all I bumped into Tony Adams a few days later having a quiet coffee and congratulated him and wished him

147

loads of luck for the FA Cup. That was a boiling hot day, and what with those goals and all the partying it wasn't for a few days that I realised what had happened, and the boys had won the Double.

VIJAY SINGH

A passage to India

When I was a young child I always wanted to paint an elephant in the Arsenal team colours. My father used to take me to the cinema and seeing elephants being painted once, I made the decision that one day I would travel to India and paint an elephant.

In 1991 I finally visited India but left disappointed after six months – having not been successful. So in 1993 my dream came true, and I was the happiest man in the world. Having travelled over two hundred miles through Northern India to buy the non-toxic washable paint, I was in Rajasthan with my elephant.

ABOVE

Vijay in his element.

STEWART TAYLOR

"I'll be there when Jensen scores"

What is it, exactly, that defines a hero? For some, such as Bergkamp, Kanu and Brady, it is pure footballing genius. Others such as Charlie Nicholas – Arsenal's first fashionable footballer for more than a decade – have relied almost entirely upon their charisma, a quality which renders them apparently immune to the wrath of their football public. Then there are Adams, Wright, Merson and Limpar – the players who made it into our hearts through a cocktail of both character and ability.

But for others the ingredient is more elusive and difficult to define. What, for example, was the making of Johnny Jensen?

Admittedly, Jensen never quite reached the heights of adulation afforded Charlie Nick, but he arrived at Highbury in the summer of 1992 with comparably high expectations. Jensen was, after all, the attacking midfielder the world had witnessed scoring Denmark's first goal in the 1992 European Championship final against Germany. Unfortunately, though, that goal helped set JJ up for failure in English football as it presented us with a completely false impression of Jensen the player and could not have betrayed his footballing character more. It was the total eclipse we now expected to see every day.

By the end of his second season at Arsenal, 1993–94, Jensen was still awaiting his first Arsenal goal. He had by now become almost a footballing caricature, trivialised but idolised on the terraces and in the fanzines – a man hell-bent on scoring from whatever range, anyhow. The bookies were enjoying a field day as Jensen sympathisers squandered their money each week. Season ticket holders behind the Highbury goals became increasingly nervy and generally refrained from adding their voices to the calls for Jensen to shoot whenever he got the ball – the Dane almost always obligingly letting rip. The sight of JJ looking despairingly to the heavens as another attempt made row Z was by now all too familiar and rather comically sad. Surely his day would come.

As the end of 1994 approached, Jensen, though now the proud owner of a 1993 FA Cup winners medal – was still goal-less. Then, on New Year's Eve, Arsenal played host to QPR.

As we filed into Highbury, there was nothing obviously peculiar about this game, certainly nothing to hint at the miracle we were about to witness. Arsenal were caught in a period of indifferent form, standing ninth in the Premiership, and they began the game in keeping with their current form (and the miserable weather) by going behind to a Kevin Gallen goal after only three minutes.

But then, 61 minutes later, something extraordinary occurred. John Jensen picked up the ball on the left-hand corner of the QPR area. Not surprisingly, at twenty to twenty-five yards out, he took aim and shot at goal. But something was different. This was a delicate, swerving shot, the like of which we had never seen from Jensen before. The world seemed to stop spinning as 32,393 spectators watched as the ball turned towards and then into the back of Tony Roberts's net.

After two-and-a-half years and 98 games Johnny Jensen had scored for Arsenal. And it was a beauty almost worth waiting for. It was a curler Michel

Platini would have died for, not the blaster à la Stuart Pearce we had all expected. Jensen went mad in front of the North Bank, the T-shirts came out of storage and there it was in the Sunday papers as confirmation – "Jensen 64 mins".

I have seen some monumental goals in my time as an Arsenal fan. Some are remembered for their sheer drama, such as Michael Thomas's winner at Anfield in 1989; others – like Dennis Bergkamp's hat-trick goal at Filbert Street in 1997 – for their brilliance of execution. However, I can think of only one other goal which has been as agonisingly awaited as Jensen's, and that was Charlie Nicholas's first strike at Highbury against Birmingham two days after Christmas 1983.

Unfortunately for Jensen, the general inadequacy of Arsenal's performance that day stole some of his thunder, Arsenal slumping to a 3–1 defeat. Jensen's moment of inspiration was, in fact, a rare highlight in what turned out to be a disappointing season. Arsenal eventually finished a poor twelfth in the league – their worst finish for nineteen years – and we all know too well who had the last significant kick of the season in Paris. And by then, to top it all off, manager George Graham – a name with which Jensen's was by now unfortunately inextricably linked – had departed in disgrace.

By the end of the 1996–97 season Jensen had also moved on, returning to Brondby with an Arsenal hit-rate of a goal every 137 appearances.

It is, on reflection, a shame that Jensen's Arsenal career has been dominated by the bung scandal, which eventually brought Graham down, and his goal mouth impotence, rather than the effective performances he consistently put in for Arsenal during his spell at the club. The greatest disappointment of all came in May 1994 when an injury denied Jensen a place in the European Cup-Winners Cup Final against Parma in his home town of Copenhagen. No other Arsenal player, though, had made more of a contribution towards getting Arsenal to that final than Jensen, with some outstanding performances in the earlier stages, particularly in Turin and Paris.

John Jensen was never going to be a Rocastle, Limpar or Overmars, but most of us didn't know any better. But what we did get was a loyal, dedicated player, a Patrick Vieira without thrills, a player who could always be relied upon to give 110 per cent. Johnny Jensen was a man not easily discouraged and on 31st December 1994 at nineteen minutes past four he got his reward.

GEORGE KAKOURIS

Wonderful, wonderful Copenhagen

The first time I ever watched Arsenal play was the 20th January 1990. My dad
had taken me to Highbury to see us play against Tottenham. Tony Adams
scored the winner from an obscure scissor-kick. One–nil to the Arsenal, and the
papers said "Donkey wins the derby", but I didn't care. This was Arsenal and I
was hooked.

In the season of '94 we found ourselves in the Cup-Winners Cup. I had been
to all the home European encounters that season with my dad. Watched us
struggle against Odense, then destroy Standard Liège, win a great tactical
battle against the Italians of Torino, and finally overcome PSG. Now the final
was here, against top class opposition, Parma of Italy. Nobody gave us a
chance, but I had two tickets for the final.

My accomplice for the trip to Denmark would be my cousin George. An
Arsenal fan through and through, and someone who knew what following
Arsenal was all about. He had been at the final against Valencia in 1980, when
we drew and lost on penalties. He told of how we had been missing Rix and
Brady and after the match he had been distraught. The anger inside was so
much he had not been to another Arsenal game for three years.

I just thought to myself, it couldn't happen to him again. This time he would see us triumphant. Though to be on the safe side, passing a wishing well at the airport, I thought of George as I made a wish and flicked in my coin.

We both took our seats at the Parken Stadium thinking we were back at Highbury. The ground was just a sea of red and white. It actually resembled Highbury in its layout, and we sat in the West Stand centre block, with the North Bank full of Gooners to our left.

Arsenal had been severely weakened through injuries and suspensions. Out went Wrighty, the legend, the goal-scorer we so badly needed. Johnny Jensen was injured, even Hillier and Keown were out. The grafters, the man-markers, where were they? Instead we had Selley and Morrow contesting midfield. Merson and Davis completed the midfield, with Smith and Campbell up front.

The Italians at the time were blessed with the silky skills of Brolin, Zola and Asprilla. But at the back we were solid – Adams and Bould the giants at the centre, Dixon and Winterburn down the flanks, Seaman in goal with broken ribs and pain-killing injections.

Everyone knew the odds were stacked against us. I knew George Graham had done his homework. Benfica taught us a lesson in European Football two seasons earlier – he had learnt a lot from that defeat and this time his troops were ready. So flood the midfield Graham-style, we may not have the skill to match, but we have the grit, desire and determination to beat them.

As the game kicked off the first chance fell to Parma, Brolin going close. Their danger man, though, was of course Zola, especially at free-kicks. At that time he had a 1:3 success rate from free-kicks. Oh dear, how many would he have that night – too many.

In the twentieth minute there was a goal. It didn't come from Zola, but from Arsenal. Dixon took a throw down the right. One of their players tried an audacious overhead kick clearance, but it fell to Smith, who took it on his chest and volleyed home a left foot drive, in off the post. It all happened in slow motion for me, the ball nestled in the net and we all went absolutely crazy. That was the goal we so badly needed and now that we had it we were not going to give it up easily.

Smith, our top scorer in our championship years, had been suffering since the arrival of Ian Wright. Smith was now the hero, and he deserved it. The goal would have only been bettered if Johnny Jensen had got one back in his home town, but who cares, it was 1–0 to the Arsenal and still seventy minutes to go. By half-time I had lost my voice completely, but the score remained the same. The second half seemed to go on for an age. As the seconds ticked by, we were getting closer and closer. We could smell victory, it was within our sights. The awesome defence held on and the tactical genius of Graham had triumphed.

The final whistle blew to a tremendous sense of relief and overwhelming joy. Once again the Arsenal had succeeded where so many said they would fall. One–nil to the Arsenal, my wish had come true, "Wonderful, wonderful Copenhagen…"

FERGUS VENENCIA

The Grand Tour

This photograph will always remind me of the carnival atmosphere of that fantastic night at the Parken Stadium, Copenhagen, in 1994.

For me personally it really was the culmination of the complete European tour, which had actually started in Copenhagen for the Odense game. We then headed for Liège, Turin and Paris. Then found ourselves back in Copenhagen for that great night.

I will always remember after the in-ground celebrations had subsided walking from the stadium. There was much back-slapping and shaking of hands, mainly due to a sense of relief, of achievement, and knowing that all the travelling and expense had been totally justified.

ABOVE

On high in the Parken Stadium.

ANDREW GEORGOPOULOS

Following the flag

I have many memories from Arsenal. This photograph is of me and a friend, Nicolas Charalambous. We both grew up in Holloway. Travelling to Europe with Arsenal has been fantastic – I have visited such sights as Copenhagen '94. I

remember Jonathan Pearce from Capital Gold Sports mentioning the flag live on air. He said: "As we look around the Parken Stadium there is the St George's flag from Holloway." To have the flag mentioned was brilliant and having won was even better, as I had thought I would never witness Arsenal winning a European trophy in my lifetime.

RYAN CHAPMAN

Still a swearword

Aged only nine years, I remember being excited and extremely confident as we travelled over to Paris by Eurostar and soaked up the atmosphere there. All the Gooners around us were in a good, cheering mood. Walking to the match with thousands of other excited fans is an experience never to be forgotten. It was so exhilarating to be part of it. We were in a magnificent stadium, (not as good as Highbury of course!), one hour before kick-off and the number of waving flags was phenomenal. We sat behind the goal to the right, with an exceptional view.

Real scored first. My heart sank and so did I, sitting down with my head held in my scarf. I managed not to cry, but thinking back I don't know how I didn't, because I even cry now, over four years later, when I think of it.

Later on something happened that would be very near the top of any list that would contain the most exciting moments in my life – the Gunners equalised! I remember almost dying with excitement. A total stranger picked me up and

ABOVE

Andrew and Nicholas display the celebrated flag.

RIGHT

Ryan in Paris for the Cup-Winners Cup Final, 1995.

spun me round, and totally in another world I kissed someone without knowing what I was doing or knowing who it was that I had kissed. With a couple of minutes to go, I was thinking about extra time and the dreaded penalty shoot-out but also praying Arsenal would score and none of that would be needed. Then the nightmare occurred, a goal was scored but not for Arsenal – Zaragoza clinched it with a murdering lob from way out, and worse – the scorer was a former Spurs player! His name is still a swearword in our house. Almost numb standing there, staring into mid-air, it was the first and still the only time in my life that my heart was broken. I tried not to cry, but after one tear rolled down my face the rest started to flow. I recall throwing my cap down into the walk-way below and thinking how wrong people are when they say that football is only a game. They're crazy, footy's life!

PAUL NAPLETON

Ian Wright, Wright, Wright!

The game when Ian Wright finally became Arsenal's all-time leading goalscorer was on a beautiful Saturday afternoon, 13th September 1997. Bolton

BELOW
*"Ian Wright, Wright,
Wright!"*

Wanderers were the opponents, and hopes were high that Wrighty would finally get the all-important goals.

Despite going behind early on, the Gunners fought back – Wrighty slamming home an effort which he celebrated as if he'd broken the record of Cliff Bastin – in fact, he'd just equalled it. He didn't have long to wait – Wrighty scored his second with a virtual tap-in after Vieira had slipped the ball across the goal.

He'd done it!

Wright took off his famous Number 8 shirt to reveal a vest saying "Just done it – 179". The crowd went wild, celebrating his glorious moment. "Ian Wright, Wright, Wright," we all roared for what seemed hours. This joy at going down in Highbury history was clear to see, and it was fitting for Wright to grab his third for a wonderful hat-trick in the second half – Arsenal eventually winning 4–1. Arsène Wenger deliberately substituted Wright late in the game to allow the crowd to worship their hero one more time – even the Bolton fans cheered him off the pitch.

It was a great game, and a day that no Gunner will ever forget.

SOPHIE SMITHER

In the pay of the Devils

It wasn't always easy being an Arsenal fan at Manchester University, but it had its moments. Arsenal have given me many great memories over the years, but the nature of this one during the second Double-winning season will be hard to beat.

When I started at University in 1996 I joined the University branch of the St John Ambulance. I always liked voluntary work, and a first-aid qualification is always useful to have. Then there was the matter of "free football matches and concerts" which also attracted me. To be honest I don't know why the organisation is not more popular!

In the 96/97 season I was not fully trained in time for the Arsenal match at Old Trafford, so I missed it – no great loss, as we were unlucky to lose by a Nigel Winterburn own-goal. When the fixtures for the 97/98 season came out, the first thing I looked for was Manchester United (A). There it was – 14th March – perfect. The fixture fell during term-time, and was far enough on through the year for me to get to know the people at Old Trafford.

As a qualified first-aider every week I had the choice of whether to go to Man United, Man City or Stockport County. I usually went to the latter two, because they are nicer teams, and the atmosphere is a lot friendlier. Old Trafford is just so huge. At Maine Road and Edgeley Park there was also the fact that my first-aid post was outdoors, so I could have one ear on the St John radio and one on the football commentary telling me how Arsenal were doing.

I did have to steel myself, though, and went to Old Trafford quite regularly. I needed to become a familiar face. I was usually put in a first-aid room, usually at the top of the giant North Stand. I always accepted this, as I wasn't upset at not being able to see the game. The radio reception was not always great in there, though, so I had to find stewards who would tell me the Arsenal score, and you couldn't trust them…

Anyway, it soon became clear that whenever I was at Old Trafford, Arsenal never lost (the losses of the Double season all came while I was at the other two grounds) and this was a superstition I liked. From Christmas onwards I turned up regularly at Old Trafford and each time I'd say "Don't mind where I'm stationed, but come 14th March I want to be pitch-side". Everyone knew I was an Arsenal fan and I was setting myself up for a big fall, they thought.

The day arrived and is one always to be cherished. I'd toyed with the idea of wearing my Arsenal shirt under my uniform, but with a shirt, jumper and coat already on, this would have been too many layers. I did have my scarf on though, discreetly around my neck, but there if you looked. We had to get there ridiculously early as it was a morning kick-off and we are required to be there two hours before the start. As officials of the stadium we get to wander round bits the general public don't get access to.

Sadly on this day I did not see any of the Arsenal team up-close and personal. As soon as I arrived in the control room I was asked which corner of the pitch I wanted. This was a big dilemma. The NE and NW corners get you on television as they are opposite the cameras, the SW corner is next to the tunnel and the SE corner is in front of the away fans. I ended up in the NE corner, which was perfect. I can see myself every time I watch the Boring Boring Arsenal video. It was a great position.

Our boys warmed up metres from me, and I could hear the Arsenal fans beautifully as they out-sung the home supporters throughout. In the first few minutes of the match Lee Dixon almost fell in my lap. It was great.

As first-aiders we are supposed to maintain a professional image and not scream or swear at events on the pitch. This was very hard that day, but I was on a post with two Man Utd fans and they too were finding it hard to stay calm. Fortunately the thousands of United fans behind me were too engrossed to notice me leaping up and getting excited about Arsenal, or else I may have been lynched. Half-time arrived and Arsenal were in control but not in the lead, and it was clear Marc Overmars was having the game of his life.

ABOVE
The scoreboard tells the story.

Early in the second half I actually had a casualty to tend to. This is what we are there for, after all, and I couldn't very well say "sorry, watching the match". It was a young girl with a nosebleed, so it was just a matter of getting her sitting right, reassuring her and filling in the necessary paperwork. All this could be done with one eye on the game, whilst her father never took his eyes off the pitch. I returned to my corner position and began thinking about a draw.

Substitutions were made and then on the 81st minute the moment arrived. Marc Overmars picked up the ball, metres away from me, and finally put it past Schmeichel. It was right in front of me and I could not have had a better view from anywhere else. Marcy, Dennis and Nic all celebrated right in front of me. The defining moment of the season, and I had seen it. I hadn't even had to pay for the privilege!

It took every ounce of me to try and stay calm and seated but inside I was going mad. The next ten minutes were the slowest of my life and I remember turning round to take a photo of the scoreboard, and then just after the final whistle went. By then I could not contain myself any longer. I leapt up in joy hissing "Yesssssssss". Just in case any hard United fan noticed this, I quickly pretended I'd got up to check the equipment and stretcher. They were too shell-shocked to notice me dancing a silly, happy jig.

We have to wait until every last fan has left the seats, and this of course took an age because the Arsenal fans didn't want to move. While everyone else moaned and grumbled I went and stood in front of them, soaking it up and waving my Arsenal scarf. Don't expect they noticed because they were all deliriously happy, like me. In the control room the atmosphere was very quiet and I just walked in and said "Why so sad?" and spent all the clearing-up time and mini-bus journey back grinning insanely and whistling the tune of "One–nil to the Arsenal".

It was by some way the best duty I ever did. As a TRS member, I would never have been able to get tickets for the match. As it was I saw the turning point of the season from one of the best positions in the stadium and it hadn't cost me a penny. That afternoon I was supposed to go on and help at Stockport but I was too hyper and had to phone every Arsenal and Man Utd fan I knew.

We are given money to cover travelling expenses for duties at Old Trafford, and the £6 I received for 14th March was the cream on the cake – I was given money to watch my team win and put them on course for the Double. Does it get better than that?

I spent the money just under two months later. Manchester United cash was used on 3rd May to buy a programme and a flag as I saw Tony Adams lift the Premier League trophy at Highbury.

ROBBIE KELMAN

From Highbury to Bondi

I arrived in cold, wet London from Australia in mid-1995, bereft of a stable place amidst the cultural storm around me. Moving to Highbury changed all that. Football saturated the streets of this North London town and I was swept up in the exuberance for the Arse.

It all began at an open window overlooking Highbury Park, N5. I watched the throng approach expectantly, showing great camaraderie as they bounced down the hill on a Saturday afternoon. Sections peeled off down side streets and large chunks rightly made their way straight into the Arsenal Fish Bar. Rightly, because their fish and chips and welcoming ways are the finest of any dinner in North London.

ABOVE
Celebrating winning the
Double in the Highbury
Barn.

RIGHT
Tony Homersham's
favourite snapshot:
"Patrick Vieira after the
match against Everton on
3rd May 1998 – the game
that gave us the
Premiership Trophy for the
97–98 season. He has the
crown of the trophy on his
head. For me, he really was
the King of Highbury."

It was at that window, with that view, noise, energy and passion that I affirmed my commitment to the Arsenal and proceeded to be part of an eventual historic Double year; to remind northerners that they would "never get a job"; to suggest to loads of them they weren't singing any more; to sing what can only be described as a lullaby to Dennis Bergkamp – to the tune of Winter Wonderland; to grow fondly into a placid hatred for "the scum" and stand up (regularly) to bear witness to this; to see Ray Parlour cut a swathe through a season culminating in a full 38,000 people chanting "Parlour for England" (only to see the most obvious call-up ignored by some Eileen Drewery drivel in Hoddle's ear); respond to the lone guy in the East Stand that "We are the North Bank"; and wonder how it was Tony Adams, with all his command, could possibly be two years younger than me?

What a sight and feeling on that beautiful warm summer day the Arse took the Premiership in 1998. Sunglasses, cold beer, fat white bellies, mobile phones exchanging scorelines and joy – sweating in the sun with flags and Gooners everywhere. Tony Adams taking a through ball from Steve Bould following a throw-out by David Seaman and scoring Arsenal's fourth against a stunned Everton. My goodness, what a superlative moment!

I've now moved well away from Highbury to Bondi Beach, where a scouser colleague, who somehow has got a job, plies me with *British Soccer Weekly* and videos of the one-hour weekly Premiership round-up.

So up the Arse – and I'll listen to the cheers on the ether, barefoot and sweaty. As you North Bank, East Stand, West Stand and Clock End Gooners await the magic of another London spring, with Arsenal running home (as they did in 1998) like a rabbit at the Hackney dogs.

DEMIAN LINN

Letter from America

I moved to Britain from Michigan in the summer of 1996 and one of my new flatmates was a rabid Gunner. We watched a few matches together on Sky, or rather he watched the match and I watched him as he jumped about the room, yelling, pleading, cursing, cheering and sometimes fighting back a tear in the glow of the television set.

I'd seen people who were fanatical about a sports team, and I'd been there myself, but I'd never seen people with such intense love for a game as the English have for football in general, and as Arsenal supporters have for Arsenal in particular. So when my flatmate had an extra ticket to Arsenal, I couldn't wait to experience it all first-hand.

That first game was an ugly loss to Wimbledon. In fact, the first five games I attended through the latter half of the 96–97 season and early days of the 97–98 season were all losses or draws. The first goal that was scored while I was within the confines of Highbury occurred during what would be the first and last time I ever left my seat before half-time, no matter how pressing my need to visit the loo. And the first goal I actually witnessed with my own eyes was a penalty kick, which Bergkamp sent home to salvage a draw with West Ham.

It wasn't the most auspicious way to start my career as a life-long Arsenal supporter, and I'm sure my flatmate, the sort of bloke who wears his lucky socks (clean or not) for the big game, was convinced I was a jinx. But I loved every minute of it, from the pre-match pint or two at the Highbury Barn to the walk to Highbury to the last touch of the ball at the end of injury time to watching the highlights replayed later that evening on Match of the Day.

ABOVE
*Demian takes a well earned
rest after the
Championship is clinched.*

And as the 1997–98 season wore on, my luck, and Arsenal's, began to change. I got to see history in the making; Adams, Keown, Bould, Winterburn, Parlour and Seaman, Bergkamp, Vieira, Petit, Overmars, Wright and the petulant Anelka playing some of the best football of their careers. I witnessed moments during that Double season that will be talked about for years to come: like Manu Petit's first goal in front of a home crowd, a beautiful curving ball from well outside the box, and Ian Wright, leaning out a window at Highbury waving to the crowd after Arsenal clinched the Championship against Everton. And Grant from EastEnders, waiting in a queue for fish and chips outside the ground with his son.

I learned a lot about England at Arsenal matches. The whole football-as-a-metaphor-for-life thing has been written about to death already, so I'll skip it. But I will say there's nothing quite like being the one voice that starts an entire stadium singing.

I don't live in England any more, but I think about the things I saw at Highbury all the time, and know I'll be back there again.

Now I'm one of the thousands of Arsenal fans scattered around the globe, listening for match reports on the radio, scouring foreign newspapers for results and staying up all hours to catch a rare match on satellite TV. It's easy to forget when you're sitting in the North Bank with 36,000 of your closest friends, but there's a whole world of people who would like nothing more than to be sitting right next to you.

DAVE PHOMBEAH

The sweetest of hangovers

I've been a life-long Gunners fan since the days of Charlie George and George Graham. My older brother took me to my first Highbury match, not long after the first Double season. It was a friendly against Wolves, when Bob Wilson kept goal. I stood on the North Bank and could hardly see a thing, and I think Arsenal lost. But for a young boy that first Highbury experience was exhilarating. I was hooked and forever had become an Arsenal addict.

These are a few pictures of my finest hours as an Arsenal fan. That wonderfully sunny and magnificent day – Saturday 16th May 1998. What was to follow was a wild uninhibited night of street dancing, beer drinking and good-natured celebration in and around the pubs and bars of Upper Street, Islington. Next morning I just made the victory parade, with the sweetest hangover ever. I mean, what a feeling – we had just done the Double again!

PETER BJERRE

The Wembley Stadium Mystery

This story illustrates the famous Arsenal Spirit that exists not only on the pitch but also among the supporters and the staff at Highbury. It's the story of a film lost at Wembley, which somehow found its owner in Copenhagen, Denmark, several months later.

Last year Peter Bjerre, a board member of the Arsenal Football Supporters Denmark, was among the happy supporters at Wembley when Arsenal won the Cup Final against Newcastle. He became an Arsenal fan aged 9 in 1971 and now was present when Arsenal won their second double title. However in the aftermath of the game and the celebrations taking place, he had the great misfortune to lose a film while searching for his ticket to the tube. The film he lost not only featured pictures from in and around Wembley, but also included some snapshots from the annual Danish supporters' tour to watch a game at Highbury, which happened to be a certain match against Everton a couple of weeks earlier…

This loss was discovered outside the stadium and put a slight damper on what was otherwise a perfect day. Back home in Denmark, Peter resigned himself to the fact that he was never going to see those irreplaceable photographs, when one day Kim Tvedegaard, the chairman of the Danish Supporters Club, rang. The film had been found, and was actually on the way in the mail. Peter, of course, could hardly believe his own ears, but was over the moon. What had happened?

ABOVE

Dave Phombeah before and after Arsenal complete the Double.

163

Steve Garrett, an Arsenal scout living in Belfast, found the film lying in the stand at Wembley, picked it up and developed the photographs. He then sent them to Highbury in the hope that the owner could be tracked down.

The photographs circulated in the offices at Highbury, where no-one had heard anything about a lost film at Wembley. After all, the film had no name or distinguishing marks, just the actual photographs which might have clues to finding the rightful owner. In London, difficult; in the UK, harder; in Denmark – mission impossible.

But one member of the Highbury staff spotted a face well known around Highbury, standing in a group in just one of the snapshots. That was Nick Glancy. Nick runs the small news-stand next to Arsenal station. He checked the photographs, all of them, but could only recognise one person – his friend and fellow Highbury resident Tony Wood. When Tony's wife Liz passed the news-stand, Nick gave the film to her, and Tony continued the detective work by checking all the pictures for people he might know. Then luck struck, Tony recognised his good friend from Denmark – Kim Tvedegaard.

He dispatched the photographs to Denmark and Kim recalled that Peter Bjerre had lost his film at Wembley – could this be the roll of priceless

RIGHT

Home at last – one of the missing photographs.

memories? For Peter, miraculously reunited with his
film, this was the perfect illustration that there really is
something special about Arsenal, its staff and its
supporters.

The crucial event that had made this detective
work possible was a meal eaten before the Final by
the Danish supporters, along with Nick and Tony, at
a local curry house. They had then, by good
fortune, joined the Danes for a rather important
photograph.

ABOVE
*Kelly Shearsmith and
friends celebrate the
Double in Leicester Square.*

ANTHONY ERRINGTON

The big match finally arrived...

I was overjoyed when reading a small article on the centre page in the Arsenal
Newsletter asking members of the Junior Gunners to take the opportunity of
becoming a ball boy or girl for the forthcoming season. I was ecstatic, as I
knew this was my only chance to meet the Arsenal team, the very team I have
supported from a tender age. But would my mother agree? What about my
homework, my piano, my reading – as if these were the only things that
mattered. But what about me? What I like and what I enjoy? For days I had
pleaded with her to let me apply, promising I would do what she had asked. I
was exhausted when she finally gave in. So I applied and awaited the invite.

Excitement and apprehension took over and I had absolutely no control. One
hundred and twenty-six people turned up for the trials, all of whom were
fighting for a place in the squad of twenty ball boys/girls. They varied from nine-
year-olds to fifteen-year-olds. The trials lasted the whole day with a short
interlude for lunch – it was tough work, but I survived. Somehow I had an eerie
inner feeling that I had done well and would be chosen as one of the squad
members. I had driven everybody including the dog mad in the household. But I
wasn't going to know until two weeks later.

Every day I had come back expecting to find what I was longing for. But that
very day was such an exhausting and boring day at school, and I had
completely forgotten about the letter. I walked into the house and as soon as

my mother appeared from the breakfast room, I guessed that there was something she was hiding. I ripped the letter from my mother's hand and hurried to my bedroom. I did not want to show my disappointment if I had been rejected. My mood changed dramatically from being very low to being on a high. It was my turn to scream. I rushed down the stairs bumping into the banisters while the dog joined in, barking, wondering what the commotion was all about.

My dream had come true. I had been chosen to represent the ball boy squad for the new season. I was over the moon, and speechless for the rest of the day. As I lay in my bed that evening, my eyes were fixed onto the white glassy mantelpiece where all the Arsenal figures and photos were grinning at me. I had grinned back, sure I finally had the chance to meet my idols, and nobody was going to snatch this chance for me.

First of all, there was going to be a meeting with Sue, the manager of the Junior Gunners, explaining all the rules and regulations, what was to be expected of us. We were given some time to get acquainted before training on the pitch. Wow! I was on that pitch, the pitch my idols had been treading and where they had scored numerous goals. The pitch was so fresh, so well kept, no sight of a dandelion. Martin, our coach, a fat cockney who loved his football, taught us the do's and don'ts. There was an irrational glee on everyone's face. It was some sort of achievement, something we could add to our CV. To my astonishment, the rules were pretty strict. We were not allowed to talk to the players, or even touch them. I raised a brow and thought how petty it was.

Before leaving we were each given a pre-packed kit sponsored by Nike to try on, which included: blue tracksuit bottoms, two black and red raincoats, a blue coat, two white T-shirts, two woolly hats (for the very cold evenings), a pair of black gloves, two pairs of socks and a pair of trainers. They were to remain in our lockers until the last game of the season.

My friends were happy for me. I was to become their reporter. For the next eight months football was the main topic at school and, unfortunately for my mother, it applied at home too. She could not escape the subject. Within a couple of weeks of my teaching she was able to follow a match on the TV. I was proud of myself – we were sharing the same cheers.

LEFT
*Anthony with the Charity
Shield and Premiership
Trophy, 1998.*

The big match finally arrived. A date not to forget – Monday, August the eleventh. What a frantic morning that had been, for me and everybody else. I was like a restless flea until I was on my way to the underground. It was only a couple of stops, but I looked nervously at my watch during the journey. Like the rest of the squad, we arrived far too early and sought refuge in the Arsenal stand, holding our bags of chips, while exchanging our anticipation of the game. We were all geared up in our new attire waiting for Martin for further instructions.

We lined up in the dugout, a tunnel leading to the changing rooms where the players were. We joked merrily, wondering who would be the unlucky soul to trip on the steps leading on to the pitch. Did the others feel the same way as I did, like one of the players, even though I was contributing a tiny part in this important match? As we descended on to the illuminated pitch, the crowd roared, sending a chill down my spine – I felt my hair standing on end. The evening was about to prove itself. What would be our fate that evening against Coventry City?

All the ball boys and girls were in position when the players made their appearance. What an ovation from their fans! I stood up and joined in. Ian Wright, the player I admired until he left for West Ham, was within reach and yet so far because of that stupid rule. The whistle blew and the game to follow was quite hot. I was on the alert all the time, and I had to remind myself to concentrate on my new tasks. It was fun and very gratifying when the crowd actually cheered when I caught the stray ball. How delirious! When Ian Wright scored, I stood up to cheer with my arms waving frantically, but suddenly remembered Sue's words. I felt embarrassed, dropped my arms and sat down as quickly as I could, hoping Martin or Sue had not witnessed this faux pas. The match was easily won with another goal from Ian Wright. The atmosphere was indescribable. I was part of it this time. It was real, it was live.

RIGHT

Tommy Lucy reflects on 25 years following the Gunners: "I have been lucky enough to witness some of the greatest moments in our club's history. It's not just these moments that make me proud to be an Arsenal man, it's the whole package that comes with supporting the world-famous Gunners. The Arsenal Way and Standard is still looked up to by other clubs."

During those next seven exciting months of football, I watched Arsenal lift two cups, the Premiership and the FA Cup. I purposely took David Seaman's towel, which he had left on the pitch after a game, even though I had no right to. It was something to show off and to boast about. There were times when my mother regretted her weakness for allowing me to take part. It was extra work for her to collect me after evening games. She had felt even more responsible for my safety, especially as my father was working overseas. The piano had suffered, in fact I stopped for a year. It would have been a waste – time was too limited. My mother was very upset about that, but I needed a break after seven years on the keyboard.

Today my room is littered with all the mementoes. Mementoes are on the mantelpiece, signed boots and balls have replaced my dull books on the glass display, photographs are stuck on the walls and my shirt framed. As my mother would say, "more to dust".

ABOVE

Double Gunners – twins Lorraine and Louise Haugh – with Tony Adams who is signing copies of Addicted, *at the World of Sport, 7th September 1998. "Congratulations Tony, you're one in a million."*

BOB BUSS

Just give us the facts

I am going to give you an outline of my son, and what Arsenal Football Club means to him. His name is Dane Lewis Buss, he is seven years and 10 months old, and he has just been signed as a goalkeeper for Staines Town Under-9s in the Surrey Primary League Division One. This achievement has been made possible by his observation of his favourite players David Seaman and Alex Manninger at all the home games over the last two seasons. When I say observation, he mimics every move they make which has inspired him to do well. If he continues making progress at this rate he will be a credit to any club. Arsenal Football Club has become his life. This has never been forced upon him but has become his greatest passion.

My son has a memory, but his memory is possibly an angle different from those others you have received. His is based on word memory, and by that I mean, on request, he can give you the result and who scored, and in what order, from any Arsenal game, home or away, in the last two seasons. In addition to this, if there was a major event – i.e. a red card – he will tell you who, as well as the name of the referee.

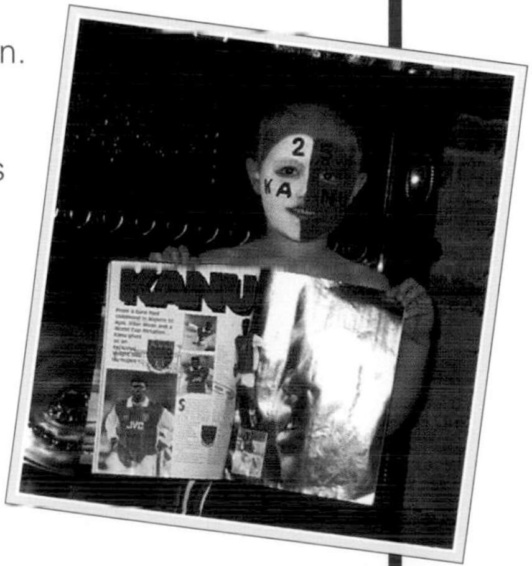

LEFT

Dane Lewis Buss displays his Kanu collection.

STEVE KELL

Pick up the ball and run

Tuesday March 9th was the date of our home fixture against Sheffield Wednesday in the 1998/9 season. After going through my usual pre-match rituals – walking the same route, buying from the lucky programme seller, etc, etc, I took my seat. As the game unfolded it was obvious that although we made all the running we were just not going to break down the Wednesday defence, even though they were not looking that good. We went in at half time 0–0.

The game needed new ideas in midfield and Emmanuel Petit was sitting on the bench after missing three games or so through suspension and injury. With 20 minutes left, Petit came on to huge applause and went straight up to Vieira and gave him the high five as if to say "Right, I'm back, so let's get into these!"

That's exactly what happened – a goal from Kanu, his first for Arsenal in front of the home fans. And a fantastic brace of goals from Bergkamp, all because the substitution lifted the rest of the team, and this is where my story really begins. About a minute into injury time Emmanuel Petit kicked the ball over the bar and into the crowd. Now in any normal circumstances I would have just thrown the ball back, but without thinking I just shoved it up my Arsenal sweatshirt and to my surprise they just threw another ball on to the pitch straight away. Then the ref blew up for full time.

I must explain what happened next because it was really eerie. This ball had now taken on god-like status on the tube, with people moving out of the way for me because they saw me carrying the ball and knew it was the match ball without being told. I am forty years old and thought that my chance of fame had passed me by – but how wrong can you be. People were asking if they could just touch the ball because of what it was and who had scored with it. (To my mind Dennis Bergkamp is the greatest player, or is on par with Liam Brady, in my 32 years of supporting Arsenal.)

When I got home about midnight I phoned all my Arsenal-supporting friends and, despite the time, most of them wanted to come round to see it. I decided that night that I had to get the ball authenticated and the only way I knew was to go to the training ground and get it signed by the team who played and scored that night. I drove to London Colney to try and find the training ground, which

LEFT
*The match ball on display
in Steve's home.*

took me about an hour, and waited and waited until a car drew up next to mine.

I was expecting to be told to leave but to my surprise Arsène Wenger got out of the passenger side and walked past my door. I quickly got out and went up to him and told him my story and he just laughed and signed my ball, then apologised to me because there were only four first team players turning up for training that day. I realised that Dennis Bergkamp was not there, so while Tony Adams was signing the ball I asked about Dennis and was told that he was back at the hotel having treatment and would not be there today.

So that was it. I had to go to the hotel to get the ball signed. I did not have a clue where the hotel was. I followed the bus for a few miles and waited for four hours before Dennis left the hotel. He signed the ball after I told him the story of how it came into my possession, and he congratulated me.

Just as a footnote, it was fantastic to meet all the people whom I pay my money to see every Saturday afternoon. I found out how appreciative they were, and how they all had time for me as well as being the politest people I think I have ever met. To this day I still get people asking about the ball. My father, who has retired to Devon, brings people with him when visiting just so they can look at or touch the ball. My son James Alex (my wife did not know at the time about the Arsenal legend Alex James) also brings his friends back to look at the ball.

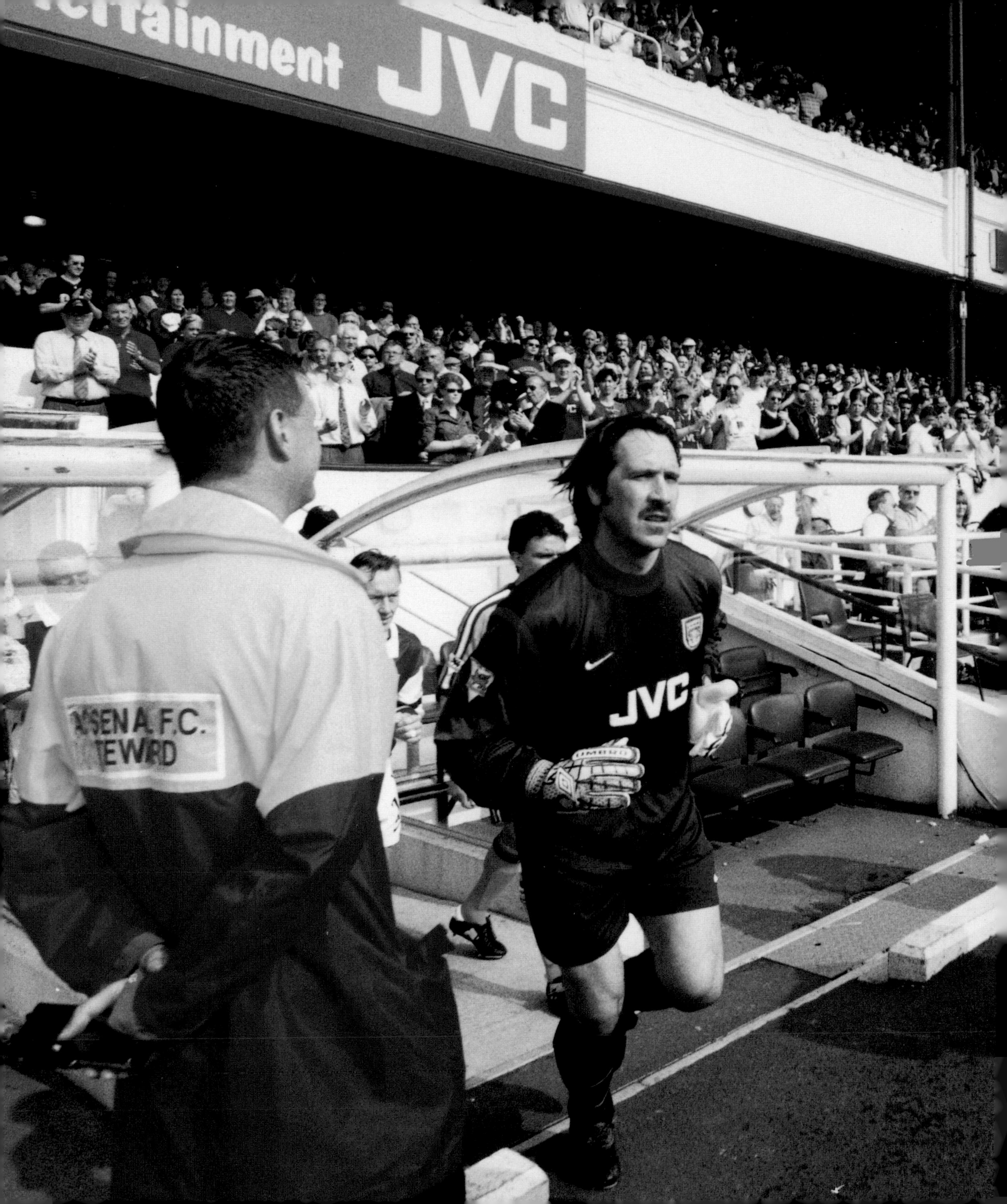
JVC
JVC

GAME ON

ABOVE

*Gunnersaurus greets a
young fan.*

LEFT

*Tony Adams leads out the
team.*

173

LEFT AND BELOW

Everybody out.

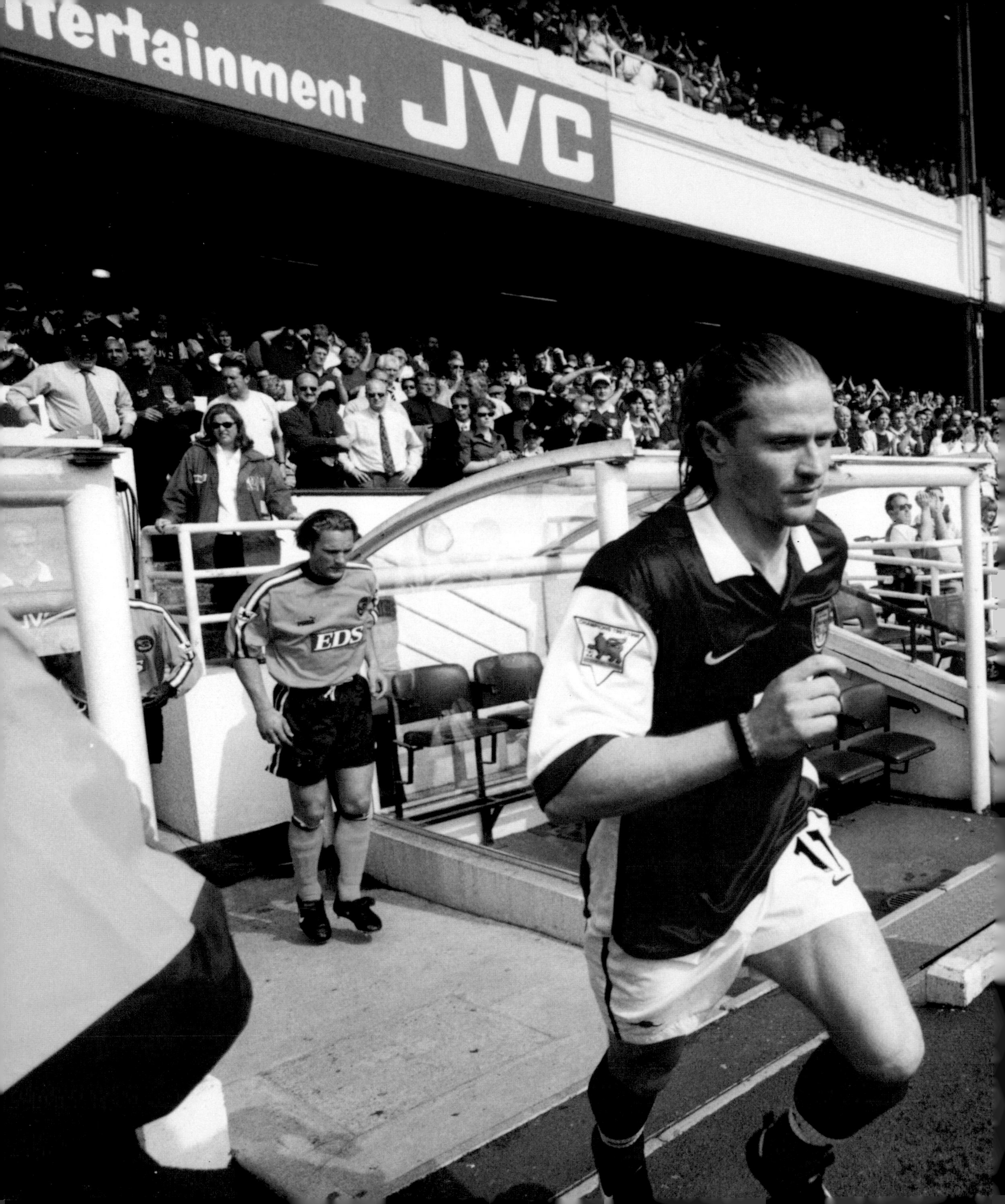

tertainment JVC
EDS

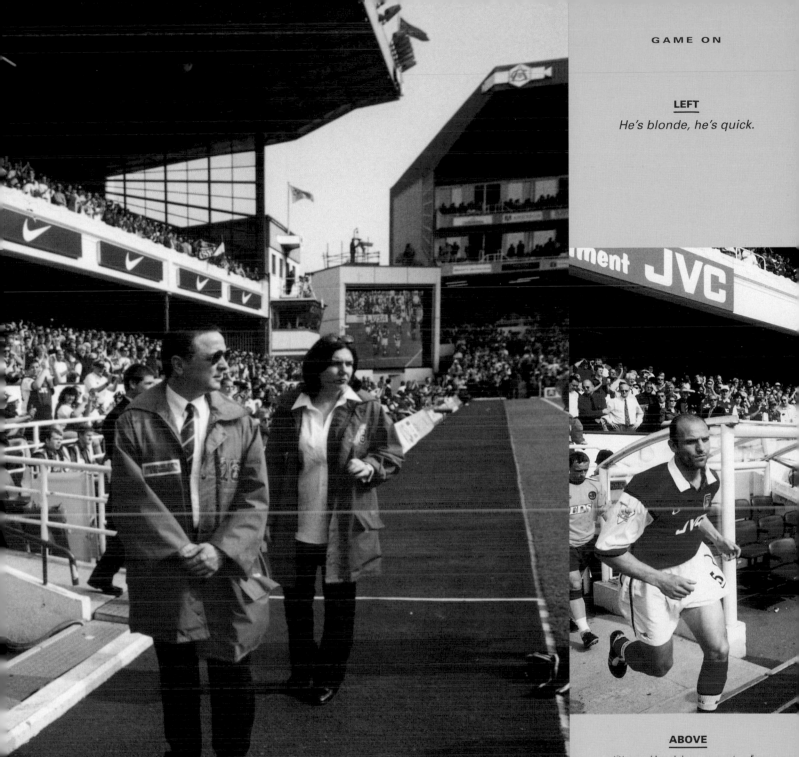

ABOVE

Steve Bould runs out – for
the last time.

177

RIGHT

The North Bank roars its greeting.

ABOVE

The young Highbury faithful.

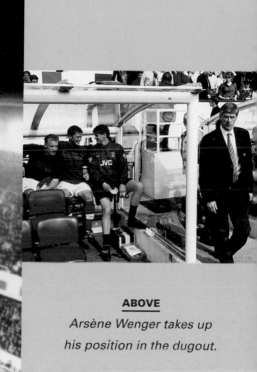

ABOVE

Arsène Wenger takes up

his position in the dugout.

LEFT

An evening kick-off, viewed

from a Clock End box.

LEFT

*Ray Parlour and Lee Dixon
– the Dreamcast in action.*

ABOVE

"Sing up for the Arsenal"

ABOVE AND RIGHT

Overmars and Petit down
but not out.

ABOVE

*"We're the North Bank,
High-bu-ry!"*

LEFT

*Lee Dixon on a run down
the wing.*

RIGHT

*Time for just one more:
the North Bank bar before
the second half.*

ABOVE

*Photographers grab a
sandwich in the film
processing room, deep
under the East Stand.*

188

LEFT

At half-time the Clock End reminds the away supporters where they are!

ABOVE

Sneaking a glimpse.

FEEDING THE INNER FAN

A cold pie and a smuggled can of warm lager was once the only hospitality you would expect watching football. Everything changes: Highbury now has one of the most luxurious hospitality suites in England – 53 executive boxes and a catering staff of 100 on match day.

All the stands have communal food outlets and bars, full to bursting before kick-off. But high above the Clock End things are very different. Fifteen hostesses meet and greet up to 700 guests, some 450 in the boxes and 200 to 250 in the Mezzanine Suite.

Yvette Brown is in charge of hospitality. She says spectators on corporate packages will be served a four-course meal in the Mezzanine Suite, "I sit down with the chef and discuss the menus, four or five weeks before a game. We have a guest speaker pre-match in the Mezzanine Suite – for example, before a recent Manchester United game I had

ABOVE
Hospitality ladies in the Clock End welcome guests.

RIGHT
Lift entrance to the West Stand Executive Suite, with the famous Arsenal carpet.

Ainsley Harriott, the TV chef, and I have only just spoken with Frank Carson about a visit. It may be a celebrity, it may be another sportsman or a former professional footballer. They are usually Arsenal fans – at one game I had Leroy of the Prodigy and Sara Cox, who are both huge fans."

Charlie George speaks before every game and is introduced by the master of ceremonies. He is asked his views on the coming game, his opinion on the

visiting team and on Arsenal, and his prediction of the outcome. "The thing with Charlie is that he is very straight to the point," says Yvette, "and he will always say what he thinks about the coming match. Then afterwards people can go up and have programmes signed – every Arsenal fan loves to meet Charlie George."

Yvette is proud to make a young fan's dreams come true. Before a game not long ago Shovell and Mike Pickering of M People hired an executive box and brought along a young Arsenal supporter who had leukaemia. He visited some of the players in one of the other other boxes – David Seaman, Paul Merson and Tony Adams – who signed his shirt. "He had been to a box with pop stars and talked to Arsenal players – that was a fantastic day for him."

The box holders are offered six different options of meal – Premier A and B (the four-course menus), the Highbury Choice, the Premier Choice, the Gunners

OPPOSITE

Lennox Lewis rushes through security.

BELOW

Chefs Malcolm Hill (left) and Steve Homer at work in the Highbury kitchen.

Buffet and a substantial sandwich basket. A comprehensive choice there, you might think, but if someone was after something specific, Yvette would do it. "If they wanted a particular bottle of wine that we don't hold in the cellar then we would get it in. One of our clients, who is a very wealthy Arab, has wine at £250 a bottle which we have to store at a certain temperature".

In the boxes the Ladbrokes staff will come round with betting slips and return to take the bets, so nobody has to leave the box. The Gunners shop, too, offers a direct shopping facility – you just phone down into the shop from the box and a representative will come up with your order.

"Arsenal TV shows the game live with all the replays on the monitors in the boxes," says Yvette, "even the controversial ones. So you don't miss anything. Of course you also get a cocktail cabinet and fridge – it's all first class treatment."

RIGHT

*"We're the East Stand,
High-bu-ry!"*

BELOW

Suker on another run.

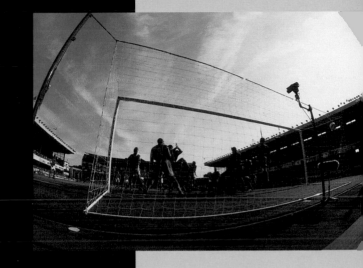

ABOVE

The ball hits top left.

OVERLEAF

It's in! The Clock End
goes crazy.

ABOVE

The East Stand is spellbound.

LEFT AND BELOW

Kanu bangs in another.

203

FAR RIGHT AND RIGHT

West Stand Lower: the view and the celebrations.

BELOW

The North Bank erupts to greet another goal.

ABOVE

Another three points...
the North Bank depart in
rapture.

RIGHT

"When's the next game?
Do you have tickets?"

BILLY PAGE

My first Arsenal game by Billy aged 7

My first Arsenal game
by Billy (age 7)

The Stadium was huge.
We saw the players come
off the bus. Everyone was
excited. When Leicester
scored I said "Arsenal!?
can do better than this!"...
And they did - Arsenal
won 2:1. we all cheered and
I stood on my chair.